Retirement By Design:

How To Pursue Your Passions, Leave Your Legacy and Live The Retirement Of Your Dreams

———————

Pamela J. Thomas

Diamond Perspectives Publishing

Diamond Perspectives
3420 Pump Road, Ste. 209
Richmond, VA 23233

First edition

ISBN 10: 1-49227-756-8

ISBN 13: 978-1-49227-7569

Library of Congress Cataloging-in-Publication Data

PRINTED IN THE UNITED STATES OF AMERICA

Table of Contents

TABLE OF CONTENTS 3
PREFACE 5
My Story 7
INTRODUCTION 9
The History of Retirement 10
Baby Boomers and Aging 12

RETHINKING RETIREMENT PLANNING 17
RETIREMENT IN REVIEW 18
Did You Know? 19
THE CHANGE 23
TRANSLATING BUSINESS SUCCESS 28
PERSONAL VS. CORPORATE IDENTITY 32
A FINANCIAL PLAN VS. A LIFE PLAN 36
THE END OF WORK 39
JOB AND IDENTITY 43
THE BEGINNING OF THE END 47
NO NEED TO PLAN 51
FAMILY TIME 55
RSS (Retired Spouse Syndrome) 56
KEEPING BUSY 60
A LIFE OF LEISURE 64
A USEFUL LIFE 68
John D. Rockefeller 68
Andrew Carnegie 69
Madame C. J. Walker 70
WOMEN DON'T RETIRE 72

RETIRING WELL 75
REINVENTING RETIREMENT 76
Earlier 77
Active 77
Healthy 78
Financially Free 78
Experiences not Stuff 79
Work/Life Balance 79
Technology 81
Intellectual Pursuits 82

Change the World *83*
Self Actualization *85*
FINANCIAL SECURITY 86
What Is *87*
Our Worth *90*
THE SEARCH FOR BALANCE 92
Letting Go *94*
Simplicity *95*
The Value of Space *97*
The Flow *100*
THE CONUNDRUM OF TIME 103
Chronos vs. Kairos *104*
Aging and Time *106*
FINDING MEANING 110
The Inner Life *111*
The Paradox of Meaning *112*
MAKING A DIFFERENCE 115

GETTING STARTED **121**
TRANSITIONING TO RETIREMENT 122
Crossing Thresholds *123*
CREATING A LIFE PLAN 128
The Foundation Is Not The House *129*
Role of the Architect *130*
CONCLUSION 133

APPENDIX **137**
PEARLS OF WISDOM 138
Peter Drucker's Ten Life Principles: *138*
The Delany Sisters *138*
Albert Einstein *139*
Ralph Waldo Emerson *140*
ABOUT PAMELA J. THOMAS 141
More About Me *143*
RESOURCES & REFERENCES 144
Books *145*
Articles *145*
Reports *146*

Preface

You are at the pinnacle of your career. After decades developing and nurturing your career, you have met your personal milestones. You love the work you do and you care about the continued success of your organization.

However, chances are you are approaching or have already reached another professional milestone—the post-career phase of your life. The idea is overwhelming, and causes you to feel very uneasy with leaving your corporate life.

It is critical for you to have a solid financial plan. But the most important issue you are facing is "what should I do with my life now?"

Instead of being immobilized by uncertainty, you can make a different choice. Retirement is an opportunity to live your passion, refine your purpose and establish your imprint on our world!

There is no need for you to keep delaying your retirement life because you are unsure of the steps to take to have a smooth transition.

If you have been anxiously wondering about the end of your career and what's next this is the book for you.

This book is for individuals who are interested in effective and meaningful retirement planning.

RETIREMENT BY DESIGN

So many people believe they are prepared for retirement because they have saved, but once they leave their jobs they discover that they actually only have a financial plan in place. Others wait until they are forced into early retirement and suddenly realize they have no plan at all.

Are you ready to stop mulling it over and start taking the steps to design your ideal retirement life?

You need to have a solid succession plan for work but it is also critical that you have a retirement strategy that is financially secure as well as personally fulfilling and rewarding.

While planning may not sound exciting, it actually can be a highly creative process. The more successful we are in our careers, the more one-dimensional our lives become. Planning for retirement is the antidote to that, allowing us to explore long forgotten aspects of ourselves.

The truth is that you will never regret spending the time to plan before you retire, once you have left your job. The clarity of purpose and peace of mind planning provides is invaluable.

A plan can never be the final word on your retirement. However, a plan is an important launching point. The framework of a plan is an indispensible guide for navigating the challenges you will face as you transition to a new way of life.

Preface

My Story

Almost 15 years ago, I decided to step away from my corporate career. Although I had enjoyed the opportunities to travel, access to powerful people, and a substantial business network, I found that something was missing for me.

I have always had a unique worldview and marched to my own beat, and I always thought that it was one of my greatest strengths. However, I felt the corporate context did not allow me the freedom to express that side of myself.

Also, I always felt like a small part in a large machine. It was difficult to see how what I was doing made a difference. I needed to find a way to work in a context in which I felt I could have more of a direct impact on people.

While the rewards have been great, the transition from the corporate life to a more unstructured work and life was challenging and required some new skills and planning. I had an idea of what was important to me but taking those ideas and making it into a life that worked for me was NOT easy.

The corporate life has many perks and benefits. There is a team of people around you all working towards similar goals. When I walked away, that support went away too.

I had wanted independence, but I discovered

that freedom also has a price. I found I had to spend more time thinking things through and planning than previously.

It took me a number of years to figure out how to create a structure in my life that allowed me to accomplish the things I wanted to do.

In my work with clients, I have seen business leaders experience the highs and lows of the transition away from the corporate life and have come to realize two important things:

1. money does not provide meaning or purpose, and
2. any time our sense of self worth is based on anything external, rather than our internal guide, our ability to derive satisfaction from our life is limited and out of our control.

My experiences have led me to really explore, in depth, what it means to be satisfied and happy in our lives, and the differences between those of us who are coasting through life and those of us who are meaningfully engaged in activities that give us a deep and abiding level of satisfaction and purpose.

For most of us, retirement is the perfect time to take a step back and review our lives and decide what really matters to us. Although we may not have control over when or whether or not we retire, we certainly can decide how we spend our retirement years. The choices are limitless.

Introduction

> *If we would only give the same*
> *amount of reflection to what we*
> *want out of life that we give to the*
> *question of what to do with two*
> *weeks' vacation, we would be*
> *startled at our false standards and*
> *the aimless procession of our busy*
> *days.*
>
> *Dorothy Canfield Fisher*

In 2011, the first of the baby boomer generation[1] turned 65, setting into motion a demographic wave that will transform our society and economy over the next few decades.

There is an enormous global trend occurring, as life expectancy increases at the same time that birth rates are stabilizing or declining across most developed and many developing nations. This shift to an aging populace will have a far-reaching impact on our world.

In the US alone, around 80 million people will be retiring during this period. There are estimates that by 2020, 25% of all employees in the US will be at least 55 years old.

In 2007, the number of Britons over 65 exceeded the number of those under 16 for the first time in history. There are estimates that well over

---

[1] A quick note: Asia's boomers are a younger generation—those born in the 70s & 80s.

600,000 people will be turning 65 each year in the UK until at least 2018.

Canada is facing similar changes where, within two decades, it's expected that 22.8 per cent of the population will be 65 and older.

In Australia, the expectation is that over 5 million people will enter retirement over the next 15 years. And in New Zealand the population over 65 is expected to double by 2040.

Considering the potential impact of these trends on our future and our way of life, it is important to understand that retirement, as we know it today, is a relatively modern development.

The History of Retirement

Until the Industrial Age, there was effectively no concept of retirement. Individuals worked until they either got sick or died. Families were larger and more generations lived together, so the younger generation took care of incapacitated elders.

The idea of retirement was originally introduced by the corporate sector. Industrial work was physically challenging and businesses noticed a significant drop in employee productivity in middle age. So, employers decided to require their older workers to leave work, so that younger, fitter people could be hired to take their place.

Introduction

Eventually, companies realized that it was irresponsible to push older workers out leaving them destitute, so they began offering pensions to support them. Life expectancy was significantly lower than today, so the expectation was that there would be a limited number of years of support.

The Great Depression shifted the conversation from worker productivity to economic stimulus. With so many young people unemployed, offering incentive for older workers to leave was a way of providing income for more people and the federal government began developing the framework for Social Security with the Railroad Retirement Act.

World War II changed things again. Labor became scarce and employers offered employees fringe benefits as a way to attract and retain workers. Once the war ended in the mid-40s, women and older workers were asked to return home to support the return of the troops.

 A large-scale effort began to convince older employees that retirement was the reward for their many years of hard work. By the 1960's this idea had taken hold and retirement became an entitlement rather than an obligation.

Most of the changes above were vehemently resisted by the older generation. For obvious reasons, they resented not being able to retire on their own terms. So, the idea that retirement is the reward for our many years of dedicated service is a very contemporary perspective.

This history has radically shaped our ideas about retirement today. However, just as we renegotiated the social contract in our youth, we have the opportunity to create a new paradigm for aging and retirement.

Baby Boomers and Aging

Baby boomers changed the world in the 60's and 70's, there is no doubt we are going to make our mark on the 2010's and 20's.

Rock and Roll music has defined this generation. The anti-establishment message still rings true for us, although we are the establishment at this point. Having not experienced a major world war, baby boomers benefitted from peacetime and appreciate its economic and social opportunities.

We are more likely than any previous generation to have attended college. College is typically a time in which young people, who are questioning their parent's worldview, truly begin to explore alternative perspectives on life and the world.

The years since WWII can be accurately described as the age of consumerism. In this short time frame, the shopping experience has been transformed. Marketing and merchandising have given us shelves filled with previously unimaginable choices.

Do you remember Ivory soap? In those days, we had one, maybe two brands of soap to choose from. Flash forward to

Introduction

today. Now when we go to the store we have shelves and shelves of soap: bars, gels, soft soap, scented, fragrance free, aloe, shea butter, cocoa butter. The choices are almost overwhelming!

Baby boomers are the first generation to be raised with these types of options and the ability to express their uniqueness and individuality.

These choices are impressive but they have also resulted in a form of generational attention deficit disorder. With so many options available, at times it seems difficult get us to get focused long enough to create things that will have longevity.

Boomers have seen an unprecedented shift to transparency in all things. Media has transformed our way of interacting with each other. In the age of reality TV and daytime talk shows, there is no subject that is off limits.

In this day and age, we have a sense that there is no such thing as personal privacy. Think of the differences between the lives of politicians today as compared with John F. Kennedy's presidency as an example.

This generation has lived through the most transformational moment in history with scientific advances beyond our wildest dreams. Our understanding of the natural world in which we live has evolved exponentially.

Technology has democratized information. Exposure and access has allowed boomers to explore the world in new ways. We are accustomed to adapting to new information and change.

This generation has also heralded a return to entrepreneurship. Industrialization had made the entrepreneur almost extinct, as economies of scale favored large enterprises. But technological advances have once again leveled the playing field, and many retirees are looking to start businesses in their post-career lives.

With record levels of prosperity and access to debt, boomers have embraced ownership. Families used to own one house or car. Now, the expectation is that each family member will have his or her own personal vehicle. And many families own multiple homes.

This was also the first generation to have highly sedentary jobs. This and extensive medical advances has led to the development of a multi-billion dollar wellness industry, that includes fitness, alternative health and anti-aging products.

The baby boomer's obsession with youth is also a relatively new idea. In previous generations, the wisdom of the elder was coveted. Ours is one of the few cultures that actually values youth over experience.

Baby boomers are nuclear family oriented. In previous generations, extended families lived together. Grandparents, aunts, cousins all lived in the same space. Over the last 60 years or so

Introduction

families have spread out across the country, and beyond, moving for job opportunities.

The nuclear family has become more of a cohesive unit. This focus on the nuclear family has advantages, but there are also some significant disadvantages. As we age, it may be more difficult to expect extended family to care for us, when they do not live nearby.

Boomers are characteristically optimistic and believe that hard work and a positive attitude provide commensurate rewards. This generation has achieved middle and upper class status in record numbers.

In the 60's and 70's, we expected to achieve great things and did. Women's Rights and Civil Rights are part of the baby boomers' legacy. Our expectations have not changed in many ways.

Boomers are also known as the "me" generation. We expect to have everything we want. There are two sides to this. On the one hand, there is selfishness. On the other hand, we also expect the best for others and have involvement in philanthropy and social change at record levels.

Because all of our lower level needs have been met, self-actualization is a realistic goal and we are definitely looking for our personal path.

The boomer generation has been defined by the way in which we have redefined traditional values. Our generation will also be transforming what it means to age and retire.

This page left blank intentionally

Rethinking Retirement Planning

RETIREMENT BY DESIGN

Retirement in Review

*As in all successful ventures, the
foundation of a good retirement is
planning.*

Earl Nightingale

If you browse the Internet for retirement
planning information, you probably would be led
to believe that financial planning is the only
critical part of retirement planning. Most people
assume that if the money is in place the rest of it
will be a breeze.

This is not to suggest that anyone should skip
financial planning, however, it is more important
to enter retirement with a vision for your life.
Research has shown that retirees
overwhelmingly agree that money plays a very
small role in their satisfaction with their lives
after retiring.

The primary role of financial planning is to
mitigate risks, so that we do not need to be
concerned about money in our retirement years.
But finances are not the substance of our
retirement.

We all want to live a life of purpose and meaning
and at the end of the day be satisfied and
contented in our lives.

Money is not the only concern in preparing for
retirement. We also need to begin to think about
our legacy and what difference we would like to

make in the world. It is vitally important to step back and look at our lives and decide what is meaningful to us.

Did You Know?

- Most baby boomers will have 20-30 years of retirement.
- Business leaders who do not begin to plan before retiring experience a turbulent transition in leaving their work.
- The first 2 years after retirement is typically a period of marital strife.
- Retirees who are socially, economically and civically engaged live longer than those who "take it easy."
- People who retire early with no plans for meaningful & enjoyable activities have a lower life expectancy.
- 60% of retirees look for a job after retiring.
- One out of four retirees have a difficult time adjusting to retirement and experience some form of depression and 15% experience severe depression.
- Retirement is associated with an increased tendency to develop addictive behaviors, in particular alcoholism, prescription drug addiction and gambling.

The best predictors of life satisfaction post retirement are NOT financial issues—they are quality of life issues (mental and physical health and relationships with family and friends).

RETIREMENT BY DESIGN

If we approach our retirement planning purely from the financial perspective, we are ignoring the important details of how we spend our days. We can be caught by surprise at how tedious it is to pass the time with tasks and other repetitive activities.

> *Some people spend more time planning a 2-week vacation than they do retirement planning.*

Anecdotally, it does seem that the majority of people retire either unwillingly or by choice with no particular life plans in place.

We spend a lot of time creating extensive plans for our careers and families. It seems that a comparable amount of thought and energy should be put into deciding how to spend our retirement years. A financial plan without a life plan has little meaning.

Without a plan, most people languish in the first two years of retirement adjusting to the changes. We all have heard stories about people who die within a few months of retiring. It is not that retiring in and of itself is a bad thing. It is that most people need some structure in their lives.

Entering retirement with specific plans and goals gives us a framework for creating that structure. Even if our financial situation deteriorates, we still have a plan that we can adjust to fit our new reality.

If you think you don't need a retirement plan

think again…

> I left work when I could get early retirement. Since my pension and investment income would now be half of what I previously earned I scrambled to earn what I could in a small side business.
>
> But my life took a turn for the worse. Things got so bad that I would wake in the morning with depression hanging like a cloud over me before I even entertained the first thoughts of the day.
>
> I got sadder and angrier and my family relationships deteriorated. Fortunately, I had a friend, who stayed at my side and pushed me to get help.

This is not an unusual story. Retirement is a major life change. It is important to understand and prepare for the challenges that a change like this brings.

If this gentleman had taken the time to plan before his retirement, he might have had a very different experience. A detailed plan would have provided him some particular goals and objectives to keep him motivated and engaged.

Retirement is not a particular date or a party. It is a process that we all must experience in our own way. It is one of the major thresholds in life that we all must navigate.

RETIREMENT BY DESIGN

Most retirement advisors focus on the financial challenges of retiring. But, while it is true that money is important, it is not the endgame, money is just the means to an end.

Retirement does not have to be just an ending. It can be the most exciting and fulfilling time of our life where we do exactly what we want when we want and only do the things that really matter to us.

The Change

*When you retire, you're going
through a major life change; you
have to reorient yourself to figure
out who you are.*

—Dr. Louis Primavera

As we approach our retirement years, we begin to dream of the days when our lives will be our own. We can start each day with a clean slate and do exactly what we want to do when we want to do it. It sounds ideal. We figure all we have to do is get to our retirement with enough of a financial cushion and we will be set for the rest of our lives.

Many of us have a picture of retirement that involves us golfing, boating or some other leisurely past time in a warm climate, sipping Margaritas and watching the sun set in big comfortable lounge chairs.

I was thinking about this the other day when something struck me. Do you remember what it is like taking an extended vacation from work?

I know that for me after about 2 to 3 weeks of downtime, I start to get a little stir crazy and start to long to get back to my routine at work. This is a far more pressing issue for the average retiree.

RETIREMENT BY DESIGN

With life expectancies increasing, most of us as baby boomers will have 30 or more years in retirement. That is about one third of our expected life span.

In 1935, when Social Security started the retirement age was 65 and the average life expectancy was 62. Even if a person made it to 65, the anticipated number of years of retirement was significantly lower.

Today, we are facing the possibility that our retirement years will be as long as our working years. For some of us they may be longer. In that context, the idea of sitting back and relaxing seems less appealing. Individuals who have something meaningful to do in retirement have a higher quality and greater enjoyment of life.

It is not a good idea to pretend that your retirement years will be one long vacation. Yes, it is true that you should be able to do the things you want to do and have much more flexibility in your life. But, you will not want to live a completely unstructured life.

Retirement is the last major life transition for most of us. We typically think of the change as the physiological shifts that we experience as we enter our 50s and 60s. But we must deal with emotional, mental and spiritual upheaval. We all face a significant emotional and psychological shift.

The Change

In the process of retiring, we are in a sense mourning the passing of a major part of our lives. We can think about this in Elisabeth Kübler - Ross's framework for the five stages of grief, which describes the process that we experience as we face our own mortality. Although these stages can happen in any order, it is easiest to describe in the following sequence.

The first begins 3-5 years prior to retirement this is a time in which most of us know that our careers are coming to an end but it feels too early to spend too much time thinking about it. Some of us try to put the thoughts aside and pretend that we will be able to stay around as long as we want to work. Kübler-Ross would call this denial.

The next phase is when the reality sets in either because of a forced retirement (layoffs or illness) or because we are personally ready to leave. Either, we try to bargain away the reality of our changing life by trying to stay at work too long and clinging too tightly to our old life and habits.

Or, particularly if we are being forced out of our jobs, we also experience anger and resentment. It is difficult to accept that after all is said and done that we are at the end of the day expendable. We feel justified in our feelings, when we do not have control over when and how we leave our jobs.

Immediately after leaving work, there is a brief 'honeymoon' period, in which we catch up on sleep and do some fun things like travelling but eventually we are faced with returning to our lives.

When we realize that retirement really is not one long vacation, depression sets in, as our reality is different than what we expected. This is a very dangerous time, from which some people do not recover. Having some planned structure in our lives, can make a significant difference in our ability to move forward with hope.

At this point we are forced step back and reassess our lives and find meaningful things to occupy our time. Finally, we find a new equilibrium and from that point on acceptance for our new way of life.

In many ways this shift is similar to the transition from adolescence to adulthood. Often we see the 50 plus crowd making the same type of seemingly questionable choices in what we call a mid-life crisis.

It is normal to look back at our lives and decide whether or not we have done the things we wanted to do and set a new course if we have not. Instead of going through that process unconsciously and in denial, it is more empowering to sit down and complete a life review in a structured way so that we make informed choices.

Prior to actually retiring we need to sit down and take inventory of our life and decide what things are important to us. I read somewhere that to retire means to "re-tire" your life. That is to give your life new traction. The opportunities are endless for us to find new meaning in things that excite us, old passions that we have not had time to pursue, explore new ideas, and help the causes that stir us.

It is worth taking the time to prepare to do and be what we want in this stage of our life. In fact, with the right planning, our twilight years can be the most productive and fulfilling time of our lives.

RETIREMENT BY DESIGN

Translating Business Success

The road that a great executive must travel between the preservation and the loss of his or her identity and integrity is extraordinarily narrow and, very, very few really make the trip successfully. It is an enormous challenge.

M. Scott Peck

I am sure you have heard a version of this story before. A successful executive begins to prepare his company for his eventual departure. He finds his successor. He sits down with his financial planner and maps out his financial strategy for the next 25 years. He finally reaches his retirement date and his friends and family give him a send off to be remembered.

At first, he is enjoying sleeping in a little later and playing golf and tennis in the afternoon. He notices that his wife seems to be out a lot but doesn't think about it too much. After a couple of months, he starts to get a little stir crazy. He and his wife are snapping at each other constantly.

His business friends he used to call and have lunch are in touch less and less frequently. His kids seem to be avoiding his calls. Six months into his retirement, he is sitting at home in his pajamas all day watching TV. His wife thinks he is depressed but doesn't know how to approach the subject with him.

Translating Business Success

This story is not unusual. Being a successful executive does not guarantee a smooth transition to retirement. In fact, successful executives struggle the most with the change in their lifestyle. One of the biggest mistakes that business leaders make is assuming that navigating retirement is similar to managing their careers.

For most successful business people, their identity is inextricably linked to their work and the structures and relationships it affords them. They are accustomed to being surrounded by a group of people that respects them, attends to their needs and wants, and hangs on every word they speak. They have assistants who handle every detail, staff who respond quickly to every idea, and business associates who tell them how wise, savvy, and interesting they are.

The keys to a satisfying retirement are very different than the key skills to be a successful business executive. Ascending the corporate ladder actually requires that you edit yourself to fit in to the corporate culture. We typically have a business persona that is significantly different than our unguarded personality. Part of that process causes us to become identified internally with that corporate culture.

There is nothing wrong with corporate success, but being productive in the corporate environment is not necessarily the same thing as being fulfilled. The corporate lifestyle lends itself to a focus on external motivators. The person who is a successful corporate animal typically is motivated by the respect, praise and rewards given by others. After a while, the individual begins to associate psychic pleasure with the external signs that they have done a good job.

Retirement requires a significant shift in focus from extrinsic to intrinsic reward. While it sounds simple, this is actually a difficult transition for those who have been primarily motivated by the way other people perceive them. Competitiveness and survival of the fittest are the principles by which most corporate environments live or die.

There is a coercive force of the group on the individual. Oftentimes individuals have been so focused on external markers of success that they do not actually have a real sense of what they personally find meaningful. In fact, they have made many decisions along the way to sacrifice their personal lives in pursuit of success in their professional lives.

The corporate identity serves an economic purpose and allows commerce to progress but it does not provide higher level needs like personal fulfillment and meaning. Planning for the transition to spending more time at home is just as important as an exit strategy for the business.

People who are happy retirees are able to strike more of a balance in their lives. They find that serving others can be just as satisfying as commercial pursuits. They recognize that change while not easy is a critical part of the process of reinventing their lives for the new terrain they will be traveling.

Personal Identity

*The best time to start thinking
about your retirement is before
the boss does.*

Most executives become business leaders
because they have demonstrated a commitment
to the values and culture of their organization
that makes them, in a sense, the embodiment of
that organization. They are key to the vision,
mission and progress of the business.

Over time the leader and the organization seem
synonymous. Although in a sense the leadership
shapes the organization, the truth is that in the
life of a well-functioning organization everyone
is replaceable.

For most C-suite executives, the connection to
their business is the most important relationship
in their lives. They have invested more time and
energy at work than anywhere else. The 60-70
hour workweek has become the norm and
essential to building their reputation and
career. Their personal identity has been
primarily formed by the organization.

Their sense of self-worth is rooted in an extrinsic
reward system: the recognition of their business
peers via promotions, compensation and power.

Most business leaders do not even realize how
much their sense of self is wrapped up in their
business until that identity is stripped from

them. Upon leaving the corporation, they have little sense of who they are without the organization, structure, title, authority, perks, staff, and clients. In giving themselves to an organization, there are benefits but those benefits accrue to the organization and the title not to the individual.

Although we treat them as if they are individuals legally, corporations are not people and we cannot develop true relationships with them. An organization does not have a moral or emotional center to which we can form a real attachment.

A business has one purpose to make money and provide economic value. When we cease to be the individuals that can best further that objective, we are expendable.

Most executives find this a major shock to the system. They have been loyal to the organization and some how expect that loyalty will be returned and rewarded. What they find instead is that the business has a life without them and continues with barely a blip on the radar. And then they find that their business "friends" are really only business focused.

Once the opportunity for mutual career benefit is gone the calls stop coming. They no longer get the expense and travel budget, the invitations to speak, and the executive assistant attending to every detail. The framework of their lives is no longer provided for them.

Retiring executives experience significant stress. Strangely enough, it appears to be more stress than they experience in their high-powered careers because of the dramatic change in lifestyle.

For many business leaders and owners, they literally feel that their identity is wrapped up in their job, title and company. Without those things they go from somebody to nobody.

> I am about to retire from the military after over 40 years of active service. At my job I am General and Sir. Off of the base I am nobody.
>
> Many of my friends are already dead. I am almost 60, financially set, and my kids are grown. I've been looking for a job, but no one is interested. I feel I will lose my identity once I retire in 60 days. My wife and children are supportive but I feel lost.

In order for executives to make the transition to retirement with ease, they must step back and reflect on who they are apart from the business, title and career. The energy they directed into developing business relationships must be diverted in other directions and in order to form further interests and connections. New friendships based on other common interests must be formed.

It is critical to have something specific and significant to look forward to prior to leaving work. Hobbies and vacations can only play a small role in a fulfilling retirement. They really only hold our interest for a short period of time. The successful retiree shifts their life to focus on intrinsic rewards and the things that give meaning and purpose.

I have worked with a number of organizations that did not help their leaders make the transition into retirement. When there is not a clean and orderly break, it has a lasting impact on the legacy of the leader as well as the success of the organization.

This is particularly true where the leader was the founder of the organization and was personally identified with the organization and the brand. (Think Steve Jobs).

There are many organizations that 10 or more years later had no sense of who they were beyond the founder and because they had not moved forward the organizations almost folded.

Apple is an exception in that regard. The return of Steve Jobs set the company on a new growth trajectory. Apple's story is definitely not the rule.

Retiring will be harder on you than on your business. It is important to prepare ahead of your retirement date, so that you can have the support and resources to make this shift as smoothly as possible.

Financial Planning

> *Money is only a tool. It will take*
> *you wherever you wish, but it will*
> *not replace you as the driver.*
>
> *Ayn Rand*

If you browse the Internet for retirement planning information, you most likely will conclude that financial planning is the most important part of retirement planning. Nothing could be further from the truth.

In fact, financial planning, primarily, is a way to mitigate risks so that we do not need to be concerned about money in our retirement years. But money is not the most important aspect of preparing for retirement.

This is not to suggest that anyone should skip financial planning, however, most people assume that if the money is in place the rest will take care of itself. Research has shown that retirees overwhelmingly agree that money plays almost no role in their satisfaction with their lives after retiring.

We can view retirement planning from the glass half full or half empty perspective. Individuals who approach their retirement years primarily from the perspective of financial preparedness (glass half empty) tend to have a much less fulfilling retirement than those who focus on the opportunities that retirement represents (glass half full).

Financial Planning

The fact is that very few of us ever feel that we have enough money, no matter what our actual financial resources are. Truthfully, the entire conversation about money and retirement is geared from the start to make us feel unprepared and inadequate.

A financial plan is the foundation for our retirement. Good fiscal planning can provide us with a broad array of possibilities for our retirement years.

However, it is important to remember be clear that money is a facilitator. It is a resource, which can open doors to opportunities. But it is not the substance of our lives.

Over the last few decades we have seen many profitable industries arise to meet the needs of this generation. The financial services boom is a prime example. It is wonderful that we have access to resources and ideas that we have never had before.

Often we are in a hurry to hand over responsibility for our money to someone else: the bank, our spouse, or our financial advisor. While there is nothing wrong with seeking advice from others, at the end of the day we must take complete ownership for how we use our resources.

It is important to remember that no advisor, financial or other, can take our place at the helm of our lives. We have to know ourselves before we can create a financial plan that will serve our retirement needs.

Money can never take the place of finding our passions and living a life of purpose and meaning. At the end of our lives, our regrets will not be that we did not have enough money. Our family, our friends, our causes, our contributions and our values will be the legacy we leave behind.

These are the things that provide joy and meaning in our lives. Our retirement years should be spent in pursuit of the higher order goals and objectives.

The End of Work

Flexible working is not just for women with children. It is necessary at the other end of the scale. If people can move into part-time work, instead of retirement, then that will be a huge help.

Theresa May

Do you think that you will retire when you reach retirement age? If not, you are not alone. 83% of baby boomers say that they intent to keep working beyond retirement.

Many people put off making plans for retirement either because they do not feel that they are financially ready or because they just do not want to face the thought of retiring. They assume that they will be able to work until they are ready to leave.

There are some very encouraging demographic trends that suggest that retirees who want to stay employed may have more of an opportunity to continue to work well past the official retirement age. There is a demand for reliable, skilled employees and mature workers fit that profile well. In the 2013 Manpower survey, it was estimated that 39% of employers are still having challenges finding staff with the right skills.

RETIREMENT BY DESIGN

There is no doubt a lot of positive news for those who want to continue to work, however, the fact is that most retirees will NOT be able to stay in the high powered positions they held as long as they might like.

54% of early baby boomer retirees say that they were forced to retire earlier than they would have liked for reasons like health or job loss. It is more likely than not that you will not have control over when you retire.

Even though most retirees who are able and want to work will find work, the work is likely to be very different than earlier in our careers. Individuals who are accustomed to being in key positions may find themselves stepping down a number of rungs on the corporate ladder.

From the corporate perspective it is undesirable to vest considerable authority in individuals who are more likely to have health challenges or die while holding and important role. This can create an unanticipated cognitive dissonance for the employee.

When we have been a business leader, it can be challenging to embrace taking orders from others, particularly younger managers. It is not always easy to be a team player when you have been the team leader. For many re-entering the corporate environment will not provide the authority, freedom and flexibility desired.

The End of Work

Being employed in retirement is typically a less structured career path requiring a more flexible approach to job positions from both the employer and employee perspectives. Some companies have begun to embrace this more flexible approach because of the ability to retain intellectual capital but others will need to be converted so that enough opportunities will be available.

It is not a sound plan to depend on working in your present role, at your present pace during your senior years. While it is possible, it is just not likely that your life will remain the same in your retirement years.

Even if you are a business owner, it may not be the best thing for the longevity of your company and your legacy to remain at the helm. Succession planning is a natural part of the lifecycle of any business and must be embraced in order to ensure corporate sustainability.

Instead of running from the reality of retirement, those of us who make the transition to retirement smoothly use the opportunity to explore aspects of ourselves that have been latent because of our day-to-day lives and responsibilities.

In our retirement years, most of us want to be in the position to decide what our work looks like. The work needs to fit the individual as opposed to the individual fitting into the job.

RETIREMENT BY DESIGN

A recent study showed that 56% of working 'retirees' want to work in a new profession. Retirement can be an opportunity to try on a new identity or explore a long lost dream.

Job and Identity

> *We are human beings, not human doings.*

Who are you? How would you define yourself? For most people the answer to this question is dramatically different before retiring as compared with after retirement.

If you answer by explaining your job title, your work, your possessions, your nationality and other external things, you are not alone. We tend to use external markers to define ourselves because it helps others relate to us more quickly. When we meet someone and tell them our job title, they can relate it to the job titles of other people they know and then they can infer how to interact with us.

Most of us spend the majority of our day at or focused on our jobs. It's no wonder we start to actually believe that our identity and personal worth is based on what we do or produce. And the truth is that most corporate environments encourage this idea, because if we identify personally with the organization and work, we are more committed to our work and do a better job.

This is clearly constructive in our work life; however, the challenge comes when we are suddenly (or perhaps not so suddenly) faced with the prospect of leaving our career behind. One of the greatest challenges we face in transitioning to retirement is disorientation related to the loss of our organizational or vocational identity.

John has been CEO of XYZ Inc. for the last 15 years. He started at XYZ in his late 20's and rose through the ranks by becoming the consummate "corporate guy." In fact, the media says that XYZ has never had a stronger global presence than under his leadership. He has a team around him, but he is the guy that holds the vision for XYZ.

Then John finds himself a few years shy of 65 and the conversation during board meetings starts to turn more seriously to succession planning. He participates in this process but everyone around him is telling him "he is the company."

He starts to think that maybe he won't start planning for retirement because the company definitely needs him around. One day the Board informs him that it is time to bring in his successor and give him a time frame for the transfer of responsibility. He gets tied up in preparing for the new CEO and then suddenly he is at his retirement party.

He does some traveling with his family for a few months and returns home to discover that he has no sense of who he is. He has lost the structure of his job, the status and benefits of his role and the connections from his corporate network.

Job and Identity

For the majority of us there are 3 factors of personal identity:

1. How others respond to us.
2. How important people respond to us.
3. Feedback we have absorbed from earlier in life.

These are all external. The tendency is to base our sense of self on how others perceive us. And this can serve us well when we are interacting with others in communities. However, this is only one part of who we are.

There are other important factors that define us, intrinsic things like our fundamental nature, our moral compass, how we express our gifts and the things that make us happy and fulfilled. These are just as important a part of who we are as the extrinsic factors. These are typically less desirable in our corporate life and so we push them to the side in the interest of achieving our career goals. For people who have been highly successful in the corporate environment, it is exponentially more difficult to disconnect from our corporate identity.

In order to successfully transition to retirement, it is important reconnect to our intrinsic value system. It is in the inner journey that we uncover our "authentic selves," the self that we were created to be and our life purpose. When we step into this new "role," retirement becomes an opportunity to contribute in ways that are more about purpose maximization than profit maximization.

I am sure you have heard it said before. We are human beings not human doings. The truth is that as human beings we had value before we ever entered the job market and we will have value after we leave our careers.

All of us at a deeper level know that each life itself has some intrinsic value beyond the external appearance. Once we face the reality of our retirement, we discover an even more profound truth. Our corporate identity is only a very small part of the story of who we are and our contribution to the world.

The Beginning of the End

> *One of the many things nobody*
> *ever tells you about middle age is*
> *that it's such a nice change from*
> *being young.*
>
> *Dorothy Canfield Fisher*

For many of us, retirement seems like the beginning of the end of our lives. We all have heard stories about people who retired and within a year they have passed. It is true that retirement is a major life transition, but it does not have to be deadly.

Statistics have shown that a higher percentage of people who retire early die earlier, but the numbers are skewed because of the percentage of people who retire early because they are sick.

There is no reason to assume that early retirement equals early death. What we do know is that some people give up on life after retirement, if they do not stay active and engaged.

In a sense it is true that retirement represents an ending of one part of our lives. However, if we look more deeply we realize that is only one side of the story.

The fact is that most of the baby boomer generation will have 20-30 years of retirement. This is almost as many years as most corporate careers. Retirement is the end of our career.

RETIREMENT BY DESIGN

Retirement is also the beginning of another part of our journey.

One of the greatest gifts and greatest challenges we face during our lives is time. On one hand there never seems to be enough time to do all the things we feel we should do. On the other hand, when we have specific goals, time moves slowly. It seems to take forever to fulfill and manifest our dreams.

In retirement, we have the opportunity to truly be intentional with our time. The ebbs and flows of other people's demands drag us along on our time during most of our lives. Retirement is the ultimate reset button. We can decide to do what we want to do, when we want to do it. BUT that means we actually need to take the time to figure out what we truly want. When was the last time we truly spent some time listening to our inner voice?

Most of use busyness to avoid thinking our thoughts and feeling our feelings. The challenge for most of us is that in order to hear to that inner voice, we have to quiet our minds. When we sit quietly, we are confronted with our feelings and thoughts.

This can be uncomfortable for us. So we return to our old patterns of busyness. However, when we allow ourselves to acknowledge and experience our thoughts and feelings instead of running from them, they can be powerful tools to help us discern what things are truly important to us.

We have a tendency to want to short cut the emotional aspects of any transition, but the gift of the shift to retirement is the ability to live into the fear and love, the tears and smiles and shift our lives. Henri Nouwen says in *Creative Ministry* that, *"retirement is one of those moments to celebrate when life and death seem to meet."*

It is in these moments of emotional, mental, and spiritual tension where our greatest creative potential lies. When we do this we touch the deepest parts of us and discover the path to living a life of authentic meaning and purpose and open the door to building our lasting legacy.

It is hard to imagine after 30 or 40 years of a career that there may be alternative ways to share our gifts with the world. The temptation is to assume that staying in our existing roles is the only way to stay relevant. But it is important to remember that there is a very important role for mature workers. There is a great need for seniors to take on the role of imparting the wisdom of experience.

In traditional cultures, this gift is greatly coveted and retirement is our call to reassess the ways in which we can contribute.

For many of us our retirement years will be the most substantial contribution that we will make to our children and to the world. And more importantly, we can make our impact in a way that is most meaningful and enjoyable to us.

Retirement can be the beginning of the most creative and fulfilling part of our lives. We each have the opportunity to redefine retirement for ourselves. It is the ideal time to take a step back from busyness and decide what we truly want our legacy to be.

No Need to Plan

*In preparing for battle I have
always found that plans are
useless, but planning is
indispensable.*

Dwight David Eisenhower

One of my clients recently said to me, "It is never too early to start planning for your retirement." And what she said is true.

While we are still in the throes of our careers, retirement sounds very appealing. Being able to do what we want to do, when we want to do it. Sleeping in late and then golfing, or sailing. Getting caught up on our reading or other hobbies. Or perhaps we pursue some other past time that we enjoy. It sounds simple.

Most of us think of retirement planning as primarily creating a strategy for saving during our working years. That is a shortsighted perspective. Saving for retirement is only a small part of retirement planning. Yes, we should start saving for retirement as soon as possible. But successful retirement planning is a complex process that takes place over a number of decades.

Our 20s are a good time to develop savings habits that will support our future retirement plans. It is important to start saving as soon as possible so that we can maximize our options in the future. The longer we wait, the fewer choices we have in our 30s, 40s & 50s.

During our 30s it is important that we assess our lifetime earnings potential and make the appropriate adjustments to our savings strategy. By this time we should have a reasonable idea of what our career trajectory might be and what that means for our financial future. This is a time in our lives that is filled with new family and work obligations. Life is full of surprises along the way, but setting goals and making long-term plan can help mitigate some of those risks.

Retirement planning should begin in earnest in our mid to late 40s. In our 40s, we need to start thinking about our big picture life goals. Do we want to stay at our present job until we are 70? What are our family's needs for the next couple of decades? What types of investments will provide good risk adjusted growth over the next 20 years? Are we planning to move?

This is also a good time to do more in depth research on our retirement benefits and options so that we can make adjustments. The key is in our 40s we need to match our savings strategies to our big picture goals.

In our 50s, it is time for us to start the detailed planning. First of all, our investment strategies require another look. For many of us it is time to start moving investments to more conservative options. Investigate health care, which benefits we are eligible for and when we will qualify for benefits.

Now is the time to start thinking about what we actually want to do in our later years. What are the things that we wanted to do as a kid, but have forgotten, as our career and family have become the focal point of our lives? What places have we always wanted to visit? Do we have some island where we have always wanted to live? Or would we prefer to be near our family?

All of the above questions lead to an important point. Our 50s is the time in which we can begin to realistically assess what our retirement income needs might be. We need to know where we stand, reassess our goals, use the many financial catch up provisions, if needed, and start thinking about downsizing opportunities.

The 60s are a time to work longer, if desired or needed, to shore up our financial resources. We should also finalize our retirement income plan, investigate the optimal time to begin taking our Social Security benefits, downsize our life, and think through multiple options for the next decade. It is particularly important at this stage to have a plan in the event that corporate downsizing and cost cutting accelerate our retirement plans.

If all of this seems overwhelming and you feel far behind, don't get discouraged. I want to let you know that it is also never too late! As I mentioned earlier, we maximize our options the earlier we start, but we can live enjoyable lives in retirement, even if we don't have our plan in place early. It just takes some reflection and thoughtful strategies.

Family Time

The love of family and the admiration of friends is much more important than wealth and privilege.

Charles Kuralt

Retirement dramatically changes the dynamic of our personal relationships. In particular, our relationship to our spouse or partner has to be renegotiated. For decades, partners have been accustomed to a particular weekly routine.

With retirement, the time spent in each other's company increases. This shift in proximity can put a strain on even the healthiest relationships and will exacerbate any relationship challenges that have been unaddressed.

Both partners have to adjust to the new dynamic. The partner who may have stayed home is uncomfortable with the intrusion into his or her routine. On the other hand, the partner who has worked may not appreciate the expectation that she or he will participate in more of the household duties.

The spouse who had a work life typically has challenges initially developing new "retirement friends." He or she may become overly dependent on their spouse.

Business leaders often have another set of challenges. Successful CEOs have many perks. At work most executives are surrounded by people who respect them, attend to their needs, and respond to every request. They have assistants who handle the details and business associates who tell them how interesting they are.

Many business leaders come home and expect things to be similar to the job. They expect to be the CEO of the home. It is difficult to figure out how to handle the details of life. It can be a shock to the system to discover that your spouse and children may not always be willing or able to pick up where the executive assistant left things.

RSS (Retired Spouse Syndrome)

Some men worry about retiring because they fear their wives will control their free time and the house. They fear the honey-do list will take over their lives.

The truth is that most stay-at-home spouses don't want someone under foot, monitoring their activities and invading their space. Spouses need the same autonomy after retirement that they did before.

> There was a report a few years ago from Japan explaining how retired husbands in Japan were making their wives sick. Cast aside from the rigid corporate structures, these "corporate men" turn their management tactics on

> their spouses, *"barking orders, nitpicking every detail of dinner, demanding service."*
>
> The study found that the stress of having their husbands at home had led to a variety of ailments. Symptoms included stomach ulcers, rashes, throat polyps, and slurred speech. So many cases were diagnosed that doctors in Japan named it *retired husband syndrome.*

Additionally, "workaholics" may find that their families resent being expected to be attentive when work was more important to the partner or parent, previously. Having been too busy for 30 or more years, all of a sudden this stranger wants to know what and when things are happening.

The newly retired spouse find her or his partner out of the home way more than anticipated. The spouse is finding a way to create more personal time.

Adjusting to being at home, after a lifetime of work is not for the faint of heart. There is no easy way to make the change, it takes planning and preparation to make the transition smoothly.

The first 2 years of retirement are very difficult for most families. According to one study, the divorce rate for those over 50 has more than doubled from 1990 to 2010. What makes this more interesting is that divorce rates are dropping in every other demographic besides the baby boomers.

> *Divorcing as an elderly person*
> *is about the worst financial*
> *decision you could make"*

It is significantly more expensive to pay for separate retirement lifestyles than to share a life. Not that any amount of money is worth trading for peace of mind, but for most of us, it is very important to consider what our relationship challenges might be before our retirement parties.

We also cannot always assume our partner and children will have the time to entertain us because we have time. It is important to plan for separate interests and activities to give our families the space they need. Retirement planning requires a "separate togetherness" in which families forge a new closeness through independence.

> *He who is overly attached to his*
> *family members experiences fear*
> *and sorrow, for the root of all grief*
> *is attachment. Thus one should*
> *discard attachment to be happy.*
>
> *Chanakya*

A recent survey of retirees found that 39% of retirees find 'relations with family and friends' is most important to them compared to 19%

reporting 'physical health' and 8% 'personal finances' as being most important to them.

Clear and open communication is critical to successfully redefining our personal relationships. Creating a new process for shared decision-making helps to deepen bonds and provide a foundation for forging a new life together.

Those who love deeply never grow old; they may die of old age, but they die young.

Dorothy Canfield Fisher

Keeping Busy

"When we get too caught up in the busyness of the world, we lose connection with one another - and ourselves."

Jack Kornfield

Some of us think of retirement as the opportunity to catch up on all of the things that we have left undone over the years.

Typically, there is a good reason that we have not completed these things over the years. The truth is that they are not activities that are interesting or fulfilling for us.

More often than not we start working on the to-do list but these projects never get completed. Just because there is time to do the work does not mean that it is actually something interesting to do and so our energy and interest wanes quickly.

Instead of trying to take on busy work, it makes more sense to take the time to plan for a meaningful retirement. It is important to stay active during retirement, but it is more important that you are doing what you want to do.

If you are busy for the sake of being busy, you are like a hamster on a wheel going nowhere. Like any addiction, busyness can only temporarily anesthetize us from our fear of aging, living alone or dying.

In order to design a fulfilling retirement, we must slow down and take stock of our lives. Spending all of our energy and time on to-do lists and mindless tasks is a primarily a distraction to avoid getting to know ourselves.

> *If you only do the easy and useless jobs, you'll never have to worry about the important ones, which are so difficult. You just won't have the time. For there's always something to do to keep you from what you really should be doing....*

> *The Phantom Tollbooth*

We live in a culture mesmerized by busyness. Our Protestant ethic tells us that work and activity are virtuous. Productivity is an economic term that suggests that, if we are not busy doing something that produces something tangible, we are not doing something constructive.

Busyness is a virtue we wear to impress others. Busyness makes us seem and feel important, even when we feel little. It is also an armor we wear to keep others at a distance. It invites the false comparison of "I am more busy than you are" and therefore more important.

There is a difference between filling our time with meaningful and enjoyable activities and just filling our time.

Busyness prevents us from being connected to our own center. When we are running around doing, we do not have time to stop and listen to the voice within.

"The idlest minds are those that inhabit the busiest bodies."

Bauvard,

More is not always better. Sometimes more is just more. Busyness is definitely not always better than stillness. It is important to reflect on the areas of our lives in which more activity is really more and focus our energy and attention on those things that will truly improve the quality of our lives.

Often busyness is a symptom of us not knowing ourselves well. Slowing down is difficult for many of us because when we slow down we actually hear our own thoughts. Often we do not like what we hear.

If we can sit still through the discomfort, those initial negative thoughts lose their power and will subside.

We do not know what matters to us, and so we allow other's agendas to shape our lives. Once we enter this cycle, it becomes more and more difficult to get back to our center.

When we are busy we cannot hear what is calling to us. Retirement is a time to ask why we do what we do. Not to be cast around at the whims of other's agendas but guided by our internal compass, the source of our true creative potential.

> *Finally, everybody agrees that no one pursuit can be successfully followed by a man who is preoccupied with many things— eloquence cannot, nor the liberal studies—since the mind, when distracted, takes in nothing very deeply, but rejects everything that is, as it were, crammed into it. There is nothing the busy man is less busied with than living: there is nothing that is harder to learn."*
>
> *Seneca*

RETIREMENT BY DESIGN

A Life of Leisure

*"Work is not always required.
There is such a thing as sacred
idleness."*

George MacDonald

Since World War II, retirement has been considered a time to relax and pursue leisurely activities. Many baby boomers were raised with parents who believed that after working hard all of their lives, retirement is the time to kickback and let others take care of them.

That dream is long gone. It is clear that the generation retiring now will not have the luxury of expecting to be taken care of by others. Increasingly, aging workers are facing the reality that they cannot depend on being able to collect Social Security benefits to provide a comfortable retirement.

It is human nature to have the desire to produce what we need using as little effort as possible. Efficiency at its heart is grounded in this idea. The more efficient we become, the more time we should theoretically have to pursue the things that interest us. However, leisure without the balance of work or activity is dull.

*"Work is a blessing. God has so
arranged the world that work is
necessary, and He gives us hands
and strength to do it. The
enjoyment of leisure would be
nothing if we had only leisure. It is*

A Life of Leisure

the joy of work well done that
enables us to enjoy rest, just as it is
the experiences of hunger and
thirst that make food and drink
such pleasures."

Elisabeth Elliot

The western concept of leisure traces its origins to the Greek word *schole,* "a state of being free from the necessity to labor." *Schole* was the search for the wisdom of life. Leisure was considered the most desirable use of one's time. Interestingly, this same word is the origin of the word school.

Retirement can be a time to "return to school" with our own agenda and interests. With the benefit of wisdom and experience, the pursuit of education and other learning is very different than in our childhood and youth.

We have a unique opportunity to pursue knowledge in a way never seen before. Technology has transformed access to education. Now we can attend lectures and take exams from the comfort of our homes. Ivy League schools are offering online classes. Community colleges have local and online offerings. There are no limits to the possibilities.

Traditionally, the senior years have been considered a time of little activity and even frailty. While it is true that there is no way to reverse the process of aging, the advances in medical technology have given us a new perspective on what it can mean to age. In previous generations it might have been considered reckless to exercise in our senior years.

Now we understand that activity is a key to a high quality of life. Inspiring seniors like the Delany sisters, who took up yoga in their 60s and continued to practice headstands well into their 100s, help us to broaden our thinking about aging.

Some have suggested that leisure serves no productive purpose. We now understand that time for recreation and play actually opens the door to more creative thinking and pursuits. They go hand in hand. Leisure without the activity of creating is less than satisfying. Likewise work without time to relax and rejuvenate is drudgery.

> *Leisure is only possible when we are at one with ourselves. We tend to overwork as a means of self-escape, as a way of trying to justify our existence."*
>
> *Josef Pieper*

Historically, leisure activities are one of the ways that we demonstrate our social standing. In the past, only truly wealthy people had the resources to engage in leisure.

Baby boomers are the first generation to have the majority of their cohorts experience leisure. We now have the expectation of time for leisure on weekends. This exposure has made, as is often the case, leisure less of a status symbol and less desirable than it was for previous generations.

We can reclaim the ancient meaning of leisure for ourselves. There is no reason that leisure has to just be defined as not working. Instead we can think of leisure as the freedom to not have to labor as well as the freedom to pursue interests beyond a purely commercial purpose. With that definition, leisure can encompass many activities: sports, studies, volunteering, all fit the bill.

Leisure is a powerful source of creative inspiration. We baby boomers have the opportunity to redefine retirement as a time when we find a more healthful balance between leisure and work. The most satisfied retirees are those who find meaningful ways to contribute by sharing their talents. But they also embrace the space that a slower pace provides as a window of creative recharging and preparing for greater contributions.

The only way to avoid being
miserable is not to have
*enough **leisure** to wonder*
whether you are happy or not."

George Bernard Shaw

A Useful Life

Life is not accumulation it is about contribution.

Stephen Covey

For high-powered business leaders, retirement feels like the end of their useful life and contribution. After a career of accolades, it seems that nothing can compare with that type of success.

The truth is that there is a long list of highly successful business executives and visionary leaders who have made their most significant philanthropic contributions in their post retirement years.

John D. Rockefeller

John D. Rockefeller had a long and controversial career in the oil industry followed by a long and productive career in philanthropy.

He and his advisers invented the conditional grant, which required the recipient to "root the institution in the affections of as many people as possible who, as contributors, become personally concerned, and thereafter may be counted on to give to the institution their watchful interest and cooperation."

After his retirement Rockefeller provided support for many major scientific and philanthropic advances of his generation: the burgeoning field of biomedical research, developing vaccines for cerebrospinal meningitis and yellow fever: the cause of public sanitation, creating schools of public health at Harvard and Johns Hopkins; and helped major international public health efforts including those to contain hookworm, malaria, and yellow fever.

Rockefeller modernized medical training in the United States, and built China's first western-styled medical school. He promoted the cause of education nationwide breaking down the barriers of gender, race, and creed. He founded the University of Chicago, and within a decade, it became one of the world's leading universities.

Andrew Carnegie

Andrew Carnegie was another of the major industrialists of the 19th and 20th centuries. He made his fortune in the steel industry.

Carnegie spent his last years as a philanthropist. After his retirement he turned his business skills, which had enabled him to create his wealth, to philanthropic endeavors and created some of the most enduring institutions in America.

His believed that, "he who dies rich, dies disgraced." Carnegie considered his greatest accomplishment to be that he lived his own philosophy of distributing wealth within one's lifetime.

RETIREMENT BY DESIGN

Madame C. J. Walker

Madame C. J. Walker is best known for being the first female self-made millionaire in the US. As a widowed mother, this daughter of former slaves transformed herself from an uneducated farm worker and washwoman into one of the 20th century's most successful, self-made women entrepreneurs.

After she retired from the day-to-day operations of her company, she joined a group of Harlem leaders who visited the White House to petition for Federal anti-lynching legislation.

Madame Walker trained and taught other black women how to become entrepreneurs. She also convened one of the first national meetings of businesswomen in the country.

She contributed to many causes including the NAACP, YMCA, schools, orphanages, and retirement homes.

There are countless contemporary examples of similar types of significant contributions: Sir John Templeton, Bill Gates, George Soros, and Brooke Astor to name a few. With information and technology fortunes being built daily, more people are entering the ranks of the wealthy than ever before.

These are all individuals who made fortunes and found ways to give to the greater good after retiring. Our own gifts may not be as grandiose but are nevertheless important and may have a significant impact on the lives of others.

We all have an innate need to be a part of something larger than ourselves. The amazing thing about looking for ways to contribute, no matter how small, is that the smallest gesture can have a significant impact on another person and through them, leave our legacy to the world.

When you cease to make a contribution, you begin to die.

Eleanor Roosevelt

Women Don't Retire

As more women have entered the workforce over the last 40 years, we are facing the same challenges that men face. While there are very many similarities, men and women do have different experiences in their careers and in retirement. Although we do it differently, women also struggle with the transition to retirement.

Here are some facts:

- Women live longer than men—on average 3-6 years. So we will probably have to plan financially for a longer retirement. For many of those years women are likely to be on their own.
- Women tend to earn less than men and participate in the work force less steadily, resulting in lost income and job seniority.
- Women are less likely than men to fully participate in a pension or profit-sharing plan.
- When women do build savings, they tend to borrow against their balances or use them when they switch jobs or need money.
- In 2007, men age 65 and over had an average income of about $34,000, while women averaged about half that income ($18,000).
- According to a 2012 report based on Current Population Survey data, in 2010, 26.3 percent of older women relied on Social Security for 90 percent or more of their family income, compared to 20.2 percent of older men.
- In 2010, an estimated 17 million women received retired worker benefits, 2.3 million

received spouse benefits, and 4.4 million received survivor benefits.
- Poverty rates for female seniors are almost double those of male seniors.

Perhaps, the most important difference between male and female retirees is that women tend to earn less over their lifetime because of the responsibilities of child rearing, extended family care and pay inequality. This has a tangible negative effect on their anticipated retirement benefits.

Women who do not have corporate jobs also go through a process of retiring, including the transition from raising a family to being an empty nester and when their spouse retires from work.

Depending on a spouse for income has its own challenges. Spousal benefits are reasonably good, but it gets more complicated if there are multiple marriages and families. During the last two decades mid-life divorce rates have more than tripled, putting more women at risk of poverty in retirement.

It is important that women who have not worked outside of their homes maintain a strong partnership with their spouse as the couple navigates their retirement years together.

> I am a widow, and I am struggling with strong feelings of desertion and lack of self-worth at the moment. I used to live for the weekends when I could sleep late. And I did, with no problem. Then I

decided to retire at 65 and now I wake up at 8 and stare at the ceiling filled with anxiety on the verge of a nervous breakdown. I thought would LOVE to be a free spirit and enjoy life. Now, instead of enjoying life, I am depressed!

I consider myself to be an intelligent person who knows that I should do something part time, start a little business on the side, or volunteer. But, the problem is I can barely get myself out of the house.

I haven't heard from my co-workers, who I thought would be calling me to get together after work. They have just moved on. I also did this with retired co-workers.

The loneliness of widowhood is one side of the coin. The other side of that coin is that many female retirees face is bearing the burden of extended family responsibilities. As part of the "Sandwich Generation," women entering retirement are likely to have both children and parents that require care.

Our retirement does not necessarily look the same as men but women face challenges in making the transition to retirement. We women, as traditional caregivers, have to reprioritize our lives putting ourselves in the front of the line. For many women retirement is an exciting new journey, where unencumbered by the needs of others, we can take a deep dive into our creative genius and make our mark on the world.

Retiring Well

Reinventing Retirement

*The boomers' biggest impact will
be on eliminating the term
'retirement' and inventing a new
stage of life... the new career arc.*

Rosabeth Moss Kanter

The baby boomer generation has been defined by the way in which we have redefined traditional values.

With between 8,000 and 10,000 people turning 65 every day, according to the Pew Research Center, it is certain that the baby boomer generation will continue to have a major impact on the global economy and social fabric. We can also expect that the definition of retirement will look very different than previous generations.

Dr. Ken Dychtwald has found in his work that,

*For a majority of today's older
adults, the retirement dream is
proving to be an unhappy and
diminished period of life that is
too often characterized by social
isolation, loneliness, inertia, a
sense of personal diminishment,
and financial dependency.*

Today's baby boomers are no longer looking at retirement as a time of relaxing. They are trading in the old paradigm for a new set of rules that provide something more exciting, challenging and rewarding.

For many the retirement years are the chance to chart new directions, to embrace *the Third Age*. They can finally pursue their passions and dreams and live their lives to the maximum.

What exactly does this new retirement look like?

Earlier

This generation of retirees, despite the best efforts of marketers and financial services organizations, is less concerned with security than previous generations. That is because they see more potential and opportunities for their later years.

Many boomers are looking for opportunities to retire early from their corporate careers, so that they can pursue other interests.

Active

Baby boomers are generally active and intend to stay active. Whether it is travelling, volunteering, gardening, renovating, golfing, cooking or exercising, retirees are seeking out activities they enjoy and can continue to enjoy for the 30 or so years of retirement.

Most recently, there is an emerging trend of new retirement developments that are labeled virtual retirement or "active adult" communities. Boomers who want to pursue outdoor and fitness activities will find a group of like-minded cohorts and the facilities to pursue their active lifestyles if they are willing and able to pay the price.

The amenities in these developments look very different than a typical retirement community. Tastes have changed considerably and the amenities are different. There will be a little less focus on golf and more on active pursuits and socializing.

Healthy

The fitness craze of the last 30 years has had a significant impact on the health and expected longevity of the boomers.

This new generation is entering their retirement with the intention of having and maintaining a high quality of life in their senior years.

They spend record amounts on wellness and alternative medicine.

Another take on this trend is the relatively new brain fitness industry based on scientific studies that show brain function is improved by finding increasing challenges and exposure to new things.

Financially Free

The boomer generation is more financially free than previous generations. This does not necessarily mean that we are extremely wealthy (although they are more prosperous than previous generations), but that money is not what matters most. We have not experienced hard times like the Great Depression, and therefore, do not have a deep-seated fear of poverty.

Experiences not Stuff

Baby boomers are looking for new and exciting experiences. This generation has lived through the most transformational moment in history with scientific advances beyond our wildest dreams. Our understanding of the world has offered new insights into what it means to be a human being.

For most of us, unchartered terrain that is ripe for exploration is our inner world. Many of our generation are seeking experiences that test our boundaries of what we know about ourselves.

Work/Life Balance

Record numbers of baby boomer have decided to work after the reach retirement age. In a recent study more than half of those surveyed said that they intended to keep working after retirement.

Many boomers associate their self-worth with their job and after retiring they lose a sense of self-esteem. Although the freedom of retirement sounds appealing, once they retire they feel unproductive. Continuing to work gives them a sense of wellbeing and purpose.

Some are continuing to work in order to shore up their financial resources. But more are actually looking at retirement as an opportunity craft their own job description and do work that they love. They are also staying to maintain a social connection.

Retiring can be very isolating. Upon retirement, boomers often lose touch with fellow workers.

Generally, boomers are in relatively senior positions on their jobs. While there are a lot of perks of being in senior management, it comes with a commensurate level of responsibilities.

An ideal shift for many boomers will be to find a way to use their experience and skills in other contexts. For many companies, retaining the intellectual capital of the older generation is appealing as well. But for corporate boards there is also the concern of the transfer of intellectual capital to ensure the longevity of the organization.

Traditionally consulting roles have been offered to retirees, who still have relationships with major clients or some other important role. Corporations are beginning to investigate more structured flexible work options for more retirees to help with the retention of intellectual capital.

A recent study by AARP showed that 16.4 percent of the 5.6 million baby boomer workers aged 50 and older, are self-employed. What's even more interesting is that one-third of those who are self-employed started their businesses after age 50.

We have a role to play in helping with this shift. We have an opportunity to take leadership and instead of trying to hang on to our jobs for dear life, we can initiate the process of transitioning knowledge by allowing younger leaders to do the day-to-day work as we create more flexibility in our lives.

For a better quality of life, it is critical to shift our pace at work. Do we really want to work 10 to 12 hour days in our 60s and 70s? Using our experience and expertise in a flexible work arrangement allows us to contribute and retire. It provides a work/life balance, so that we can enjoy our work, family and recreation like never before.

Work is love made visible. And if
you cannot work with love but
only with distaste, it is better that
you should leave your work and sit
at the gate of the temple and take
alms of those who work with joy.

Kahlil Gibran

Technology

Recent advances in technology have changed every thing from dating and traveling to learning and starting a business. Baby boomers have not ignored this trend. The late boomers were the first generation to be required to take computer science in school and they have never looked back.

With the advent of the personal computer, things like writing a letter or a book on paper are almost a thing of the past. More than half of boomers are using social media for both professional and personal needs. It was estimated that 83% of boomers were Internet users in 2011.

Baby boomers may be a little behind the curve on embracing the Internet but retirement will provide the opportunity to really explore and get up the learning curve quickly. We will find new ways to integrate technology into our retirement lives. Just as technology has democratized information, we expect retirement lifestyles and interests to become increasingly accessible.

Connectivity through social media has and will continue to change how we form and maintain relationships. *Facebook* groups and other online social networks will facilitate reconnecting with friends from the past and create a new mode of retirement networking.

Intellectual Pursuits

Khan Academy, *Coursera* and *Udacity* are changing the face of education. Baby boomers will have an unparalleled opportunity to pursue higher learning at almost any price point and even from the comfort of their homes.

Some boomers will still opt for the traditional classroom as a means of broadening their social networks. Research has shown that an actively engaged mind is critical to brain health. Ideas being developed to serve this aging population will likely have an impact on how we educate young people in the future.

Passion

In this day and age when most of us find ourselves reinventing our careers at least 2 to 3 times over our careers, retirees often return to the job market to pursue their passion. We've done the "get ahead" years and are through with that. Now we want work to match our skills and strengths with our passions. We want to find happiness in our work as well as a paycheck.

Retirement should be the time in which we are free enough to follow our long lost dreams and interests. Allowing our imaginations to consider any and all possibilities for our retirement is an empowering tool for making the shift.

Change the World

Volunteer organizations will see boomers knocking at their doors to contribute time and money. Even during their careers, this generation has been involved in philanthropic endeavors in record numbers. The extra time afforded during retirement will only make those ties deeper.

What is more interesting, is that a recent survey found that about half of baby boomers polled in the United States would prefer to give their wealth to address social and environmental concerns rather than pass it down to their children.

Many wealthy boomers are concerned that their children are not adequately equipped to manage their inheritance and want to ensure that they leave the impact they intend. They also believe that it is important for each generation to earn their own wealth.

Between now and 2050, an estimated 41 trillion dollar wealth transfer will occur that may be funneled into transforming the social sector.

Baby boomers, as the free love generation, realize that it has a moral, social, and most importantly an economic interest in helping to transform our communities. Although we have philanthropic intentions, we also have a strong interest in evaluating and measuring the impact of our investments in the social sector.

The burgeoning field of Social Finance is likely to be a major beneficiary of this trend. The search for ways to use financial resources to deliver powerful social and environmental benefits, and in some cases, a financial return is an important new dynamic. Social Finance encourages positive social or environmental solutions at a scale that purely philanthropic endeavors and traditional investment cannot achieve.

Self Actualization

Known as the "me" generation, there is no doubt that baby boomers will pursue any and all avenues to find our own path. Personal fulfillment will be a paramount goal as those over 50 begin to transition to the Third Age.

As opposed to previous generations, who had a cookie-cutter idea of what retirement would look like (golf, vacationing and relaxation), boomers will be taking on retirement on their own terms.

Retirement is a point in our lives in which we can truly become all that we desire. But it is important to seek sound advice in order to draft a personalized plan for the retirement of our dreams.

Financial Security

> *The word **secure** comes from two*
> *small Latin words: **se** meaning*
> *"without" and **cure** meaning*
> *"care"—being without care,*
> *freedom from anxiety.*

> *Eric Butterworth*

Are you seeking or have you achieved financial security? What do the words mean to you? Do you know someone who is financially secure?

Financial security is not a real thing. Security cannot come from or be based on financial things.

Money is energy and therefore has an impetus to flow, transform and change. If we are looking to money (or any external thing) for security, we will always be left wanting.

The fact is that security is the result of an orientation to life and the world. It is a by-product of our understanding of ourselves and our relationship to the Universe. When we understand our connectedness to each other and to the Divine, there is a feeling of protection and care that can be a true source of security.

To be without care is a state of mind and a choice. It has absolutely nothing to do with what we have, it reflects who we are. Our sense of security provides clear and direct insight into our understanding of the world in which we live.

Financial Security

Do we believe that the Universe is a place of only struggle? Or do we believe in something beyond us that provides all we need with ease and grace? Do we believe that people with the external trappings of money and assets are those who are truly blessed? Or do we believe there is more to living the good life?

Culturally we see some very confusing messages about security. We have been told that if we have enough money and things that we will finally obtain a sense of security. The financial services industry has encouraged us to believe that we must be dependent on professionals to make sound financial decisions.

The fact is that it is critical for each of us as an individual to take responsibility for the wise use of our financial assets. In order to experience a sense of security about our financial condition, each of us must embrace our fiscal responsibility with knowledge and joy rather than with fear and trepidation.

When we begin from a space of being *secure*, our finances, in fact, all aspects of our lives fall into order. That does not mean that money comes easily, or can be used wastefully, but that we have *our daily bread*. From that center, we attract all of the resources we need for the work we are called to do.

What Is

I have discovered that for most of our financial journey we deal with what we wish we had or did not have in our lives. How many times do we sit and daydream about what we would do if we had more money? Or wish that we knew how it would feel to not have so many bills to pay?

We either look forward to the promise or challenge of the future, or we long for or run from our past. It is truly a rare gift to find someone able to sit comfortably with *what is* in his or her fiscal world.

In all of the stresses of dealing with our finances, the truth is that at the heart all of the daydreaming and wishing is the desire to be comfortable with what is in our fiscal lives. At the end of the day we all want to be free from worry.

The revelation for me when I distilled the essence of that sentiment is that I realized that I could make the decision to be at peace with *what is* at any time I choose. At the end of the day, it boils down to a choice I can make.

Now I have to admit that this revelation was liberating and terrifying all at the same time for me. On the one hand I knew that I have the ability to make my own decision. On the other hand there was an aspect of which it seemed utterly impossible for me to be comfortable with not having enough money in the bank to pay the bills in front of me or to deal with the uncertainty of layoffs in my office.

Financial Security

After much soul searching I came back to the conclusion that I still have the power of choice.

I think it is worth talking about what the choice means. I would not say that it means taking a Pollyanna-ish approach to our financial affairs and pretending that even though we have little in the way of finances, we can buy anything we want because the money will come.

On the other hand I think that it also does not mean that we shut off and shut down all spending and completely retrench. It seems to me that this choice is really a choice to:

1. sit with the current situation,
2. see clearly *what is*,
3. ask for and accept guidance,
4. make the best decision at the moment,
5. and be comfortable with that.

Some time the guidance we receive will inspire us to move forward with ambitious plans. Even with the most exciting ideas the right use of resources is required. There is a delicate balance of holding *what is* possible with what is.

Often, restricted financial resources are a lesson, helping us become more efficient and effective stewards of our resources. It is important to understand that stewardship of resources does not mean having money to spend without discretion. It is really about getting clear about what we really need for the moment. It is the choice to see *what is*.

Our Worth

Most of us think of wealth as something that has to do with dollar signs and a number that is called our "net worth."

When we attempt to calculate our "net worth" we look at bank accounts, cars, houses, financial investments and so on. Then we subtract the money we owe other people. What is left on the bottom line is typically how we determine our net worth.

Let's step back for a moment and look at the words. We actually tell ourselves that we can define our "net worth" by material things. Of all the potential words and ways to describe our worth we have allowed ourselves to believe that things matter. The language we use to describe money and our relationship to money has a significant impact on our psyches.

It is an interesting thing that if we look up the definition of wealth on the Internet all of the definitions refer to material things. The word wealth comes from the Old English word *weal,* which means wellbeing and happiness. Do we really believe that material things have the capacity to create wellbeing in our lives? The world of things is constantly in flux. To attempt to build our sense of wellbeing on something so unstable seems foolhardy.

We all know people with large bank accounts and net worth who live with a poverty consciousness. They struggle with every dollar. Worrying about their "stuff" saps all of their energy night and day. There is never enough money.

Likewise, we all know people who have little in terms of tangible assets but live abundant lives, in which no need goes unmet. These people never seem to worry about where their next meal is coming from or how they will make it through the day. They just are.

The second is the truly wealthy person. A sense of wellbeing can only come from within. It emerges from an orientation to the world in which there is an understanding of a beneficent power that is responsive to our needs.

Money never made a man happy yet, nor will it. There is nothing in its nature to produce happiness. The more a man has, the more he wants. Instead of its filling a vacuum, it makes one. If it satisfies one want, it doubles and trebles that want another way. That was a true proverb of the wise man, rely upon it; "Better is little with the fear of the Lord, than great treasure, and trouble therewith."

Benjamin Franklin

The Search for Balance

Happiness is not a matter
of intensity but of balance and
order and rhythm and harmony.

Thomas Merton

What does balance feel like for you? It may be difficult to describe what balance feels like, but when you have balance in your life you know it.

Balance is a flow along the path of least resistance. You glow with the fire of inspiration but can also sit cool and collected in contemplative thought. You are present with the knowledge of your past and the possibilities of your future. Retirement is the perfect opportunity to redefine your search for balance.

Most of us understand balance as some form of homeostasis in which every thing is calm. This, of course, is why most of us feel balance is an unattainable dream.

In truth, balance is more similar to a flow in which energy moves freely in, out, between and around our lives.

There are a few basic characteristics of balance:

1. Balance embraces all our emotions.
2. Balance means change.
3. Balance means clarity.
4. Balance is efficient.
5. A lack of balance is a clear signal to pause.

The Search for Balance

Finding balance in our lives works best if we work from the internal to the external.

The internal factors are mental, spiritual, emotional and physical. When we find inner balance we,

- are mentally active with spaces of mental rest,
- are alive with the zeal of inspiration and engaged in the world as well as disciplined with regular contemplative practice,
- give love and receive love, and
- are attentive to our eating and exercise as well as our sleep.

When we find balance internally, the external balance comes more easily. In work, we are productive but also enjoying the journey. We can be socially active and fully engaged with our family but have plenty of personal time. Are involved in activities that we are passionate about but also take time apart.

Activity without rest is enervating and not constructive. Embracing a change of pace is critical to balance. We all need downtime to recharge and re-center. During your downtime, conduct a review of your activities. Eliminate the ones that don't enhance your life or minimize the time you spend on them.

When you find yourself feeling out of balance, pause for a moment. That's when it's time to take a "30,000 foot view" of your life, so that you can bring things back into perspective.

RETIREMENT BY DESIGN

"Your hand opens and closes,
opens and closes. If it were always
a fist or always stretched open,
you would be paralysed. Your
deepest presence is in every small
contracting and expanding, the
two as beautifully balanced and
coordinated as birds' wings."

Rumi

It is in spaces between the expanding and contracting, the activity and stillness, the mental and the physical, the spiritual and the secular that the quality of health and life is found.

Letting Go

Some people believe holding on
and hanging in there are signs of
great strength. However, there are
times when it takes much more
strength to know when to let go
and then do it.

Ann Landers

Have you ever had the impulse to purge your house? Did you notice how much better and clearer you felt afterwards? There is an energetic shift when we create space in our lives. It makes room for new ideas, passions, and even relationships.

But in order to make space, we have to be prepared to let go of things that we have held to tightly. Our beliefs, expectations, knowledge are all part of the purging process.

It can be painful to let go of the things that we think we know, the things that we believe define us. And yet that is what we are called to do everyday.

Letting go makes space for our inner wisdom to emerge and transform our lives. It brings us closer to our truth. Releasing simplifies our lives because it brings clarity and purpose. It is an invitation to a larger, more inclusive Truth.

Simplicity

To manage the storm around us,
we need to quiet the storm inside
ourselves. By doing that effectively,
we can devote more attention to
whatever we decide matters most.

Tony Schwartz

Our world feels chaotic. I don't know whether you feel the same as I do, but it seems as if time is accelerating. I know that there are still only 24 hours a day, but it seems different.

Despite the fact that I have many tools to help me get things done, there always seems to be more that needs to get done. And there is never enough time to get everything done.

Our tendency is to want to manage it all by looking out there for the latest gadget, process, or assistant. But the truth is that we can only manage the chaos out there by managing the chaos within us first.

Simplicity is a virtue.

Simplicity supports our ability to be nimble and respond quickly to change. Simple questions typically lead to the most innovative leaps in understanding. Simplicity is a key component of the elegant solution.

> *Any intelligent fool can make things bigger, more complex, and more violent. It takes a touch of genius — and a lot of courage — to move in the opposite direction.*
>
> *Einstein*

And if you are not convinced, think about some of your own experiences. In so many instances we actually seek simple answers to our questions.

> Have you ever tried to return an unwanted item to the store? Most of us get frustrated with the process of trying to get a refund on the item because the process is so complicated. But we will pay more to a store that has a simplified returns process.
>
> Think Apple! Apple computers are more expensive but its fans are loyal because from the moment you walk into the Apple Store to looking to buy a laptop until you

recycle your computer, the customer service process is simple and effective.

Simplicity allows us to carve out space, in the midst of chaos, to reconnect to our purpose and seek clarity. Space provides a foundation for prioritizing and tackling challenges.

Instead of running chaotically to put out fires everywhere, in simplicity, there is a method to our madness.

The Value of Space

Spaciousness is always a beginning, a possibility, a potential, a capacity for birth. Space exists not in order to be filled but to create. In space, to the extent we can bear the truth of the way things are, we find the ever-beginning presence of love. Take the time, then; make the space. Seek it wherever you can find it, do it however you can. Seek the truth, not what is comfortable. Seek the real, not the easy.

Gerald May

Creating space is probably the hardest thing to do for the typical overworked and overwhelmed person, but it is crucial for lowering stress, increasing happiness and encouraging creativity.

It is important to actually schedule down time, just like all of the other things we do all day long.

Make time to do nothing, but allow the space around us and radiate and expand you. Space to heal, recover, and allow for inspiration.

It is worth it to take the time to figure out what works for us. We can meditate, write, sketch, do some yoga or simply sit quietly for a few minutes each day and do absolutely nothing.

Music is the space between the notes.

Claude Debussy

Between the inhalation and exhalation there is space latent with possibilities. True power is in the in-between spaces. These are the moments of renewal, regeneration and revelation.

The spaces in our lives are similar to the winter season. In the quest for growth and understanding, we all must reach a point at which instead of resisting, we embrace the appearance of leanness. In truth, the "winter season" is a critical component of the cycles of growth and evolution.

So often we fill our time with doing: shopping, driving, exercising, playing, etc. The stillness of winter provides us with the ideal opportunity to sit still for a moment and just be. Somehow the quiet makes space for clarity that busyness cannot.

The barren season in our lives is a wonderful time in which to reassess what things are really important to us and which things just consume our resources (time, energy and money) but provide us with little in return.

It is interesting that most people, when they are forced to cut back on expenses, discover that much of what they believed were critical expenditures are hardly missed at all, and add very little that is meaningful to their lives.

At the end of the day we all want to experience joy, peace of mind, and purpose in our lives. Another pair of shoes or a fancy car has little to contribute to that quest. For most of us the more things we have, the less peace of mind we experience.

We must never forget that behind the appearance of barrenness of winter is the preparation for the appearance of spring. Without the period of rest and renewal, new growth is lackluster. The winter season is potent with potential (*pun intended*).

The space for creativity and possibility is just as important as the phases of development, growth and harvest. As we sit in our "winter" experience, can we take the opportunity to look inward for where we can release old ideas, emotions and activities that are no longer serving us? At the same time, can we also look for what new is trying to bubble to the surface and to explore new possibilities?

The exploration does not mean to "make it happen," but just to allow the mind to travel in whatever directions seem to be calling. I invite you to embrace your unique winter experience and see what is waiting for your attention.

Margin is the space that exists between ourselves and our limits. It is the amount allowed beyond that which is needed. It is something held in reserve for contingencies or unanticipated situations. Margin is the gap between rest and exhaustion, the space between breathing freely and suffocating.

Dr. Richard Swenson

It is in allowing for space that we are able to integrate and assimilate our experiences, thoughts, feelings and intuitions. Integration implies acceptance, a whole greater than the sum of its parts, and a sense of flowing energy.

When something is added to or taken away from an integrated whole, it is assimilated over time but does not completely throw the organism off balance. Wholeness is maintained. Our sense of being whole guides us through transitions. We attract our highest and best good.

The Flow

In most things, we are told maximum effort equals maximum results. However when we begin to get glimpses into the nature of the Universe, this so-called truth is turned on its head. With flow, there is an ease with which things unfold, something that we call *synchronicity*.

When the timing is right, the right people and resources seem to appear as if by magic. This experience comes not from our "efforts" but from doing the real work of setting and holding clear and focused intentions and visions.

Most of us, once we tap into a Divine idea, get a major energy surge around it—it is inspiring. It is critically important for us to hold, but not outline the specifics, the way in which the intentions and visions will be brought into manifestation.

We find our cognitive mind wants to jump in and participate in the excitement. It immediately begins kicking into overdrive with its problem solving methods. The cognitive mind is similar to a calculator. It processes permutations and combinations of all of the information it knows to find a solution to a problem.

While the cognitive mind is an important tool, it must always be in its appropriate place. It cannot be leading the effort, although if it is following the lead of inspiration, it can be a very useful tool in manifestation.

The work of inspiration has a flow of unfolding, evolving energy that if we pay close attention; we can feel, see, hear, taste and touch. We have the ability to choose to resist or capitulate to this energy. But the interesting thing is that as human beings we have another choice—we can move from resistance to cooperation to co-creation.

We are not leaves being passively pulled along by the river currents, we have tools that we can use to help navigate a safer, more enjoyable, and most importantly more direct ride in the current. Once we tap into that stream in the larger sense, the issues of money and resources become secondary.

When we are in the flow with inspiration, what we need is provided at the right and perfect time. Not when we want it, but when we need it. Tune into the flow and find your place in the unfolding Universe.

The Conundrum of Time

Paradox is a pointer telling you to look beyond it. If paradoxes bother you, that betrays your deep desire for absolutes. The relativist treats a paradox merely as interesting, perhaps amusing or even, dreadful thought, educational.

Frank Herbert

Time is an interesting thing. Have you noticed that there is always either too much time or too little time? Rarely do we ever feel we have just enough time.

Anyone you ask would tell you that we are immersed in the experience of time and yet some scientists tell us that time does not exist or that it is a continuum.

The one thing we can say for sure is that we really do not have a strong grasp on what time actually is. Isn't it ironic, then, that we spend so much energy orienting our entire lives around our perception of time?

We feel good if we think that we have used our time productively. On the other hand, we feel inadequate or guilty if we have not. Our attitude towards time shapes many of the highs and lows of our lives.

We have our personal view of the meaning of time, that is the basis of most of the decisions we make. But on the other hand, the culturally prescribed views of time and its use tend to radically shape our personal opinions.

Chronos vs. *Kairos*

> *To every thing there is a season,*
> *and a time to every purpose under*
> *the heaven*
>
> *Ecclesiastes 3:1*

The Greek word *kairos* means time but it is a concept of time that is different than the linear, quantitative perception of time known as *chronos.*

Chronos is typically the way we perceive time. We have 60 seconds a minute, 60 minutes an hour, 24 hours a day, 7 days a week, and 52 weeks a year. This perspective on time is critical to our ability to manage the details of life. However, alone it leads to a task focused existence.

Kairos is a many-layered concept of time, which is defined by its purely qualitative measurement. Liddell and Scotts Greek/English Lexicon defines *kairos* as "in season, seasonable, happening at the right or critical time," or the "right opportunity."

According to Greek mythology *Kairos* was a god depicted as a young man with short hair in the back and a lock at the front. The lock is said to represent the opportunity to seize the appropriate moment.

The great Greek philosophers were very interested with the attainment of *kairos*, particularly within the walls of the courtroom where the word came to be a legal concept of equity.

Finding an ethical balance is a hallmark of *kairic* law. Plato stated that to make use of *kairos* a speaker must understand the Truth, know the souls of his/her audience and select the right words at the appropriate time to convey that Truth to the audience.

Many scholars have used archery and weaving as analogies to explain the concept of *kairos*. Carl Glover in his dissertation on *kairos* states that to hit one's target in archery there are many different things that must come together harmoniously and precisely to be successful.

First the archer must carefully aim and draw the bowstring; then he must pick the right time to release the bow to hit a moving target; finally he must hit a vital part of the body of his prey.

Similarly, the weaving analogy refers to the precise timing of the parting of the threads on a loom so that another thread can be woven through.

There is an implication in the concept of *kairos* of balance and harmony between seemingly incompatible features that incorporates not only timing but also correctness. It has been said that *kairos* implies "a season when something appropriately happens that cannot happen just at any time...to a time that marks an opportunity which may not recur."

The word *kairos* reflects unique moments in the temporal process—moments in which something exceptional can happen or be accomplished. It is also viewed as a time for action that has been divinely ordained. The Pythagoreans saw *kairos* as the cosmic force, which brings together polar opposites harmoniously and, thereby, creates life in the Universe.

Retirement is a time in which the delicate and intricate weaving together of *chronos* and *kairos* in our lives can make a significant difference in the quality of our lives. It can be the difference between busyness that fills every waking minute of everyday and living a truly inspired life that is personally fulfilling and leaves a legacy to our children and the world.

> *A prerequisite for a sound decision*
> *is kairos, a harmony of conflicting*
> *elements.*

> *Mario Untersteiner*

Aging and Time

As we get older most of us feel that time seems to pass more quickly. Our perception of time is that it is accelerating exponentially. Much of this is a symptom of how rapidly we have made advances in science and technology over the last couple of centuries.

> In a recent NY Times, there was a very interesting article on how we perceive the speed of time.
>
> Friedman tells us that although time seems to pass more quickly as we get older, it is in fact a cognitive illusion that we can counteract. Apparently, we perceive the passing of time as accelerating for a number of reasons including:
>
> • we experience fewer truly new things
> • our emotional state
> • our ability to focus our attention
> • our ability to remember a sequence
> • certain medications

Scientists have discovered that we must keep our minds engaged in learning and experiencing new things in order to "slow" the passing of time. What better time to do that than in our retirement years?

Most people underestimate the amount of free time they will have in retirement. We typically spend 40 to 70 hours a week working. Finding productive ways to spend that time is no easy feat.

If we do not have meaningful and enjoyable activities planned, the days can seem an endless stream of tasks and mindless work until bedtime.

RETIREMENT BY DESIGN

Each passing year converts some
of this experience into automatic
routine, which we hardly note at
all, the days and the weeks smooth
themselves out in recollection to
contentless units, and the years
grow hollow and collapse.

William James

There are two commonly used approaches to time management. The first involves detailed scheduling and planning for 15 or 30-minute blocks of time. The other end of the spectrum is the "go with the flow" method, in which the schedule is determined by the events of the day as they unfold and the whims of those around us.

Most people ascribe to one or the other of these ways to manage their time. In retirement, it is worth considering changing to some form of a blended method. We need to have some structure but not too much structure.

A broad margin of leisure is as
beautiful in a man's life as in a
book. Haste makes waste, no less
in life than in housekeeping. Keep
the time, observe the hours of the
universe, not of the cars.

Henry David Thoreau

We have the opportunity in retirement to treasure our time and use it wisely. Some will take this treasure and convert it into enervating excitement. Others will allow themselves to be bored into oblivion.

The difference is that those find joy in time will be the ones who spend time planning their retirement. They understand that it is important to strike a balance between being active and enjoying rest and relaxation. Thinking about how to do that before actually retiring is empowering.

When we learn to approach our retirement life with the same wonderment as children, we will find ourselves coming to place of peace with respect to time.

*Time is a game played beautifully
by children.*

Heraclitus

RETIREMENT BY DESIGN

Finding Meaning

*Do not go where the path may
lead, instead, go where there is no
path and leave a trail.*

Ralph Waldo Emerson

Vacation homes, yachts, gems and cars, these are all outward signs of success. But at the end of the day, there are only so many things we can buy.

Have you ever thought that maybe there is more to it all?

What if you could wake up every morning knowing that you could do something you love while at the same time making a meaningful contribution to others?

Is there some gift or message you feel you need to share with the world?

We think of our passions as things that are for us and us alone. But what if the most selfless thing that we can do is to live fully into our passions?

The truth is that when we do the things we love, we show up in the world in a different way. We are joyful. That alone gives us the ability to transform others lives. Our purpose is intimately tied to our passions.

Our passions are the things that make us joyful, irritated, angry, despondent and blissful. When the work we do is something that we are passionate about, work instead of being work becomes play.

The Inner Life

> *After all it is those who have a*
> *deep and real inner life who are*
> *best able to deal with the*
> *irritating details of outer life.*
>
> *Evelyn Underhill*

We find our purpose in the road less traveled. Most of us spend our days trying to walk in the paths of others. We want the things somebody else has. We look at the self-help guru and want his charisma. Or we look at the billionaire and long for the yachts, cars and homes. Or we look at the self-made entrepreneur and covet her success.

When we are so focused on others and their lives, we lose the ability to present in our own lives.

It is in being present in our current circumstances, that we are able to find purpose. Seeking meaning in our lives is a little like connecting dots, one-by-one to reveal a picture.

Although bits and pieces of it may come to us in an instantaneous revelation, the truth is that finding our purpose is a process. It unfolds before us minute-by-minute and day-by-day. Just when we think that we have a handle on our purpose, a new facet of our life's work is uncovered.

Amir Haque in his Harvard Business Review article reminds us that we do not have to chase our purpose. It will find us, if we take the time to engage in the deeper conversation. It is revealed to us in the things we are passionate about, the things we love and the things we despise.

In the end, our legacy has both an intentional and a spontaneous aspect. It is a powerful thing to set our intention to do something, but it is in the doing of that something that our true legacy takes shape.

The Paradox of Meaning

If you follow your bliss, you put yourself on a kind of track that has been there all the while, waiting for you, and the life that you ought to be living is the one you are living. Wherever you are—if you are following your bliss, you are enjoying that refreshment, that life within you, all the time.

Joseph Campbell

Most of us think that our passions are for our own purpose and pleasure. We do things that excite us to feed our own souls. We have been taught that we cannot make money or make an impact by following our passions.

Our family and friends tell us that following our passions is a selfish pursuit and a luxury reserved for those with extensive resources or artists. There are, however, alternative ways to think about the purpose of our passions.

Some of the greatest contributions to the world come from an unbridled passion that has been allowed to run its course.

> *I have no special talents. I am only passionately curious.*
>
> Albert Einstein

Well-known mythologist Joseph Campbell suggested that the hero's journey is to *follow your bliss.* In pursuing our passions, we connect to a larger purpose and our unique contribution to the world. We typically think of those who work from 9 to 5 as contributing members of society.

However an argument can be made that the most important contribution that each of us can make is to live more fully by sharing that which makes us feel alive. When we do the things that inspire us, move us and change us; we inspire, move and transform others and our world.

So, life, as is typically the case, presents us with a conundrum. Our most selfish pursuits (our personal passions) may be the most altruistic thing that we can do. If we want to leave a lasting legacy, the most effective way is to find what makes us tick and pursue it with zeal.

> *Don't ask yourself what the world needs. Ask yourself what makes you come alive and then go do that. Because what the world needs is people who have come alive.*
>
> *Howard Thurman*

Prioritize the things that give you joy and improve the lives of others. Let the other stuff go. You will be surprised at how interesting life can be.

Making a Difference

*The legacy we leave is part of the
ongoing foundations of life. Those
who came before leave us the
world we live in. Those who will
come after will have only what we
leave them. We are stewards of
this world, and we have a calling
in our lives to leave it better than
how we found it, even if it seems
like such a small part.*

Jim Rohn

It is a natural thing for us as human beings to desire to do positive constructive things and perhaps even be appreciated for our contributions. There is something innate within us that knows the truth that things that we do for others can have a powerful and positive impact on our own lives.

There are an infinite number of ways to make a difference. No contribution is too small or too large. In fact, one of the interesting things about the things we do for others is that we rarely ever know the full impact of our actions. Just a smile when someone had a rough day could have a ripple effect beyond our comprehension.

The global *Pay It Forward* movement that has arisen in the last decade is an example of the ways in which the baby boomer generation is embracing the idea of making contributions no matter how small.

RETIREMENT BY DESIGN

*How wonderful that no one need
wait a single moment to improve
the world.*

Anne Frank

The word economics comes from the Greek word *oikonomos* meaning manager or steward. Or in other words the science of economics is the science of stewardship. That is a slightly different spin on things than you might have imagined.

Stewardship is an interesting word in that it does not have any connotations of ownership or control. Instead it is more generally used to refer to the act of taking care of something that belongs to someone else. A steward is someone who attends to the needs of another (i.e. a wine steward or a cabin steward). In essence, it is a form of service.

Sometime over the last few hundred years, we have shifted to a perspective that economics is the science of self-interest. There is a case to be made for economics being about self-interest, but I would argue that we have completely missed the bull's-eye on our assessment of the key components of self-interest.

Greed is good, is the line from the movie *Wall Street*. We have used the work of Adam Smith, in vain, to come to the conclusion that our wellbeing can be measured in material things. So we always want more stuff and are unhappier than we have ever been.

> Prior to writing his *The Wealth of Nations,* Adam Smith wrote *The Theory of Moral Sentiments.* This is where he initially posited "the invisible hand" of self-interest. In this work, he acknowledges that because of the natural order, there a significant component of self-interest actually is connected to the interests of others. We have an innate desire to identify with the emotions of others.

In truth, self-interest has a much wider scope than money or things. The good life incorporates peace of mind, healthy relationships, fulfilling work, and "purpose and meaning." Our narrow definition of self-interest has cut us off from the planet, each other and even ourselves. There can be no doubt that it is in our self-interest to have a planet that is healthy or populations of people who are housed and fed.

How selfish soever man may be
supposed, there are evidently
some principles in his nature,
which interest him in the fortunes
of others, and render their
happiness necessary to him,
though he derives nothing from it,
except the pleasure of seeing it

Adam Smith

But we have been trained to focus on immediate gratification rather than understanding that it is in our interest to make plans for the future. We do benefit tangibly from the time we take to plan for the future of our children and grandchildren.

The questions of stewardship are radically different from those of acquisition and dominance. Instead of *how do I get?* The question becomes *how do I give of my gifts?* Rather than *how do I control?* We ask *how do I empower?* Our focus shifts from *what is the quickest way* to *what will have the most positive broad impact?*

Economics cannot only seek to answer the questions of supply, demand and price. There is the equally important question of *for what larger purpose* (or why)? Decisions must have the question of intent clearly at the center.

Profitability, while a legitimate objective, is not the only legitimate objective. Not every intention has equal value in terms our self-interest. We seem to have unconsciously selected an intention that is not really serving our greater good as evidenced by the current economic, political, and social instability.

We must ask ourselves how can we reframe the science of economics so that the measure of utility (individual and corporate satisfaction) encompasses more than just the consumption of various goods and services, possession of wealth and spending of leisure time.

Living life fully requires that we harness our life energy and consciously put it to work. Instead of narrowing the economic perspective, it is critical for our survival to broaden the scope of our work to include those things that truly represent a quality of life.

Legacy planning begins with an introspective journey. It is essentially a process of clarifying your core desires and developing tangible strategies to achieve those objectives. It is also an opportunity to reflect upon your values and ideals and impart that wisdom to future generations.

There are certain things that are fundamental to human fulfillment. The essence of these needs is captured in the phrase 'to live, to love, to learn, to leave a legacy'. The need to live is our physical need for such things as food, clothing, shelter, economical wellbeing, health. The need to love is our social need to relate to other people, to belong, to love and to be loved. The need to learn is our mental need to develop and to grow. And the need to leave a legacy is our spiritual need to have a sense of meaning, purpose, personal congruence,
and ***contribution****"*

Steven Covey

This page blank intentionally.

Getting Started

Transitioning To Retirement

*When we retire we finally have the
chance to do what we want but
lose the support of being wanted.*

Henri Nouwen

Slowing down as we get older is a natural part of life. A change in pace does not have to mean coming to a complete stand still. Retirement is our opportunity to step back and decide what is really important to us. At the end of the day, we all want to find a way to enjoy our lives.

So what are the most important factors that determine whether or not we make the transition to retirement well? We have compiled a list of the key attributes of people who are satisfied in retirement. The information below is taken from a broad selection of well-known retiree surveys.

Satisfied retirees:

- have a plan and start planning for retirement early,
- retire on their own terms,
- see retirement as a new chapter in their lives,
- plan with their partner,
- are surrounded by a close circle of family and friends,
- have a strong social network,
- are socially, economically or civically engaged,
- maintain or improve their health

- stay active with meaningful activities, not just busy,
- create some but not too much structure for their lives,
- keep searching and experimenting with new things,
- have strong intellectual curiosity,
- are not addicted to achievement and accolades, and most importantly,
- do not avoid the non-financial and emotional aspects of retirement.

Retirement is another major life threshold with the inherent challenges and opportunities.

Crossing Thresholds

And it is a liminal zone, a place where one life form begins to be alchemized into another.

Emily Hiestand

Thresholds of waiting and unknowing are everywhere in our lives and they are unavoidable. Each time we enter into *liminal* space, we leave behind our old way of being and enter into a new life. The opportunity for the new does not happen without the disruption of releasing the old.

Common *liminal* experiences occur in adolescence (the transition from childhood to adulthood), graduation (the transition to independence), a new job and career, moving to a new house or town, marriage, parenthood, divorce, sickness, and of course retirement. Each time we walk through these experiences it is natural to feel disoriented, as if our anchor has been pulled up without our knowledge

In asking what's next, we have to be careful to ask the question in the full understanding that there are many possible answers. Posing the question is opening the door to many paths. There is not a quick answer. There is a process, a journey that is being laid before us.

Change never exists in a vacuum, no matter how hard we might try to control things. There are ripple effects of even a small change that we can never predict. As much as we desire to compartmentalize the various aspects of our lives, we can never actually achieve a separation.

When we find ourselves at these thresholds, we experience a great deal of discomfort. And let's face it most of us will do just about anything to avoid discomfort. We have patterns and behaviors that we use to try to "go around" the pain instead of facing it head on and walking through it.

When we look too hard for one clear answer, we often miss the gifts and growth in the journey. The threshold to retirement is no different. The *liminal* experience is characterized by three distinct stages:

1. separation,
2. the in-between,
3. re-integration.

First, we are separated (often unwillingly) from the things we know. Breaks and break ups can be traumatic experiences, causing rifts in our relationships. But they cannot be avoided in life are necessary for our personal growth.

This brings us to a space of unknowing. We call this the in-between space, where we can no longer live in our past but do not know what the future holds. The second phase tends to be longest one, because we tend to fight it.

We want to avoid the emotional aspects of crossing the threshold. There is a grieving process that we must have. We are mourning the end of an important part of our lives.

A common reaction when experiencing the feeling of being "cast at sea," is to look for something to grab hold of quickly. When we grab from a place of fear we often will attach ourselves to destructive things. Addictions and other negative patterns tend to surface.

> (Liminality is)...*a unique spiritual position where human beings hate to be but where the biblical God is always leading them. It is when you have left the tried and true, but have not yet been able to replace it with anything else. It is when you are finally out of the way. It is when you are between your old comfort zone and any possible new answer. If you are not trained in how to hold anxiety, how to live with ambiguity, how to*

RETIREMENT BY DESIGN

*entrust and wait, you will
run...anything to flee this terrible
cloud of unknowing.*

Richard Rohr

We always have a choice in how we respond to
change. The journey is easier if we have partners
and advisors to share our ups and downs. It's
really about having the right people to help you
see what you can't see, challenge assumptions
and narrowed perspectives, discover new truths,
encourage, care and assist in any way possible to
help get you through your waiting.

The *liminal* process is similar to having a
completed puzzle and someone breaks all of the
pieces apart and turns them upside down. Then,
instead of us stopping for a moment and
reflecting, we try to put the pieces back together
without turning them right side up.

If we surrender to the process rather than
fighting it, we reach a point at which all of the
pieces of the puzzle get turned right side up
again. What emerges is a new puzzle, one that is
reminiscent of the old one, but at the same time a
puzzle we have never seen before.

It is in these threshold moments of emotional,
mental, and spiritual tension where our greatest
creative potential lies. When we embrace this
journey we touch the deepest parts of ourselves
and discover the path to living a life of authentic
meaning and purpose and open the door to
building our lasting legacy.

Transitioning To Retirement

There is another important point I want to make about liminality, and that is the mobility, or freedom of movement that comes with liminality. By freedom of movement I mean the freedom to move back and forth between states and areas.

Creating A Life Plan

*Retirement is a work in progress. I
try to figure out my day, and what
I know about myself is that I need
structure.*

Pete Sampras

Retirement is a major life transition. It is very difficult to embrace this or any change, if we step into the new life focused on what we are leaving behind us.

An inspiring personal vision gives us something to look forward to, a framework for us to move forward in our lives.

Have you ever been involved in the process of building a house? If you have you know that building the home of your dreams takes a lot a preparation and planning with a team to support your vision.

Creating a retirement plan is similar to building a house.

Building a house begins with finding an architect who can share and hold your vision and help you step by step on the path to bringing that vision into reality.

Next, you work through the details of that vision with the architect. The result is a blueprint, a visual representation that communicates that vision and keeps your team on track.

Once the blueprint has been finalized and the team has determined that the resources needed to create this vision are available, then the building starts with laying a foundation.

The Foundation Is Not The House

> *"Your house shall be not an*
> *anchor but a mast*
> *It shall not be a glistening film*
> *that covers a wound, but an eyelid*
> *that guards the eye."*

> *Kahlil Gibran*

A financial plan is the foundation for our retirement. It is critical to lay a sound foundation to have a sound structure.

However, it is important to remember that the difference between the foundation of a house and the actual living space. The foundation is not the house in which we live our lives.

In building a house, the foundation is not the first thought. In fact, if we build a foundation without knowing what the structure of the living space is, we will not have the right foundation in place to support our house.

Just as a foundation helps to stabilize the house, a financial plan mitigates some of our retirement risks but it does not give meaning to our life.

Our financial advisor is the *structural engineer* of our retirement plan, but the structural engineer actually needs guidance from the owner and the architect before beginning his work. It is critical to begin with a plan for the life of our dreams. The financial services professional can only help us achieve our goals if we are clear about what we want.

Even the best-laid financial plans may prove to be inadequate. Many retirees have discovered since the 2008 financial crisis, that the generally accepted strategies for conservatively investing for income are no longer meeting their retirement needs.

There are always multiple ways to achieve any goal, but we have to remain focused on the goal not on mistakes from the past, in order to keep our energy moving forward. Beginning with a focus on financial issues keeps us focused on the past and the challenges of facing retirement.

Retirement is a major life transition. It is very difficult to embrace this or any change, if we step into this new life focused on what we are leaving behind us. A purely financial perspective tends to cause us to place our focus behind us, on what we did not do or could have done better.

Role of the Architect

When building a house we also need an *architect* to help plan our *living space*.

*Architects take your vision and
give it form, explore its
possibilities, raise it to new levels,*

*and then integrate it into your
building site and the community
at large. They bring not only
design but solutions.*

Your retirement advisor is the architect for your
vision for your retirement—taking your vision,
giving it form, exploring its possibilities, raising
it to new levels and then integrating it into your
financial foundation and your life at large.

A good retirement advisor will:

1. help you take a personal inventory
2. support you in casting your vision, and
3. help you work through the details to realize
   your retirement vision.

A purely financial perspective tends to cause us
to place our focus behind us, on what we did not
do or could have done better. But making the
right financial choices can only be in the context
of a broader vision for your life.

Making the right financial choices can only
happen in the context of a broader vision for our
lives. Do not underestimate the importance of
having clear goals and the steps to reach those
goals mapped out prior to exiting your
business. A comprehensive retirement plan
provides the framework for making a smooth
transition to a new way of life.

Integrating all of these things into a coherent
retirement plan takes time and can seem
overwhelming. A retirement coach or advisor is

a sounding board, objective advisor and creative partner in mapping out your ultimate retirement.

Start planning for your retirement as early as possible. Invest the time and money in getting access to the resources you need to design the retirement of your dreams.

It's indeed possible to live well without a Life Plan, just as you can find your way to a destination without a map. But it is easier with a plan, and you are more likely to enjoy the journey.

Michael Hyatt

Conclusion

*The only worthy goal is to make a
meaningful life out of an ordinary
one.*

Peter Drucker

We are at the cusp of the emergence of a new way of aging and retiring. Rather than running from the word retire, it can empower us if we embrace and reinvent it. Webster's Dictionary says that to retire is to withdraw or move back. While at first glance those may seem like disempowering words, we can paint them in a different light.

From a balanced perspective, withdrawing or moving back is a power move. In the ancient martial arts form *T'ai Chi Ch'uan* power comes from retracting and absorbing the opponent's brute force. It is characterized by the use of leverage through the joints rooted in coordination and relaxation, rather than muscle tension, in order to neutralize or initiate an attack.

At its essence, *T'ai Chi* is the study of the appropriate response to external forces. It involves yielding in response to an incoming attack rather than attempting to meet it with opposing force.

According to its principles, a much more effective defense can be waged from a withdrawn stance. Moving back, as opposed to being an act of weakness, is a means of controlling the situation through creating a major shift in the dynamic of an attack.

T'ai Chi is the balance of opposites: *Yin* and *Yang*, dark and light, soft and hard. Its philosophy embraces the integrated perspective, an alignment of the inner with the outer. Inner hardness is expressed as outer softness.

The inwardly focused control allows for an unexpected shift in energy and a successful conclusion to a challenge.

There is great wisdom in giving rather than reacting to another's activity in order to gather momentum to achieve an objective. *T'ai Chi* takes great discipline, wisdom and experience to master and is considered to be an advanced martial art form.

In *T'ai Chi Ch'uan* it is said that the soft overcomes the hard, and the extremely soft becomes extremely hard. In becoming soft, we can see what is going on around us more clearly and choose a more effective response.

Retirement is our time to withdraw, and from that posture of strength, find the leverage that we can use to transform our world and leave a fitting legacy for the generations to come. This is our *kairos* moment!

*Retirement is a time to make the
inner journey and come face to*

Conclusion

face with your flaws, failures,
prejudices, and all the factors that
generate thoughts of
unhappiness. Retirement is not a
time to sleep, but a time to
awaken to the beauty of the world
around you and the joy that comes
when you cast out all the negative
elements that cause confusion and
turmoil in your mind and allow
serenity to prevail.

Howard Salzman

This page is left blank intentionally

Appendix

Pearls of Wisdom

Peter Drucker's Ten Life Principles:

1. Find out who you are.
2. Reposition yourself for full effectiveness and fulfillment.
3. Find your existential core.
4. Make your life your endgame.
5. Planning doesn't work.
6. Know your values.
7. Define what finishing well means to you.
8. Know the difference between harvesting and planting.
9. Good intentions aren't enough; define the results you want.
10. Recognize the downside to "no longer learning, no longer growing.

The Delany Sisters

A word to older folks:

1. Keep your own calendar. The most important thing in your life is your time, and nothing will make you feel as helpless as having other people run it for you.
2. Manage your own money, but be careful about it. Pay your own bills and balance your checkbook for as long as you can. When the time comes that someone has to take a hand in your finances, make sure you understand everything he does. If other people take charge of your money, it's easy to lose control of your life.

3. Have your own doctor, who answers to you. If you don't, when the time comes that you get mixed up with hospitals, they'll treat you like a fool. You're bound to lose your health at some point, but you don't have to lose your dignity, too.
4. Don't depend too much on any one person. If you have a lot of helpers, you can be sure that someone will always be available when you need it.
5. Don't be too proud to accept your limitations. The hardest thing is discovering that you can't do everything the way you used to. But make sure you hire folks who do what you want. It's still your house, and you're still the boss!

Albert Einstein

1. "I have no special talent. I am only passionately curious."
2. "It's not that I'm so smart; it's just that I stay with problems longer."
3. "Any man who can drive safely while kissing a pretty girl is simply not giving the kiss the attention it deserves."
4. "Imagination is everything. It is the preview of life's coming attractions. Imagination is more important than knowledge."
5. "A person who never made a mistake never tried anything new."
6. "I never think of the future – it comes soon enough."
7. "Strive not to be a success, but rather to be of value."

8. "Insanity: doing the same thing over and over again and expecting different results."
9. "Information is not knowledge. The only source of knowledge is experience."
10. "You have to learn the rules of the game. And then you have to play better than anyone else."

Ralph Waldo Emerson

1. "For everything you have missed, you have gained something else, and for everything you gain, you lose something else."
2. "To be yourself in a world that is constantly trying to make you something else is the greatest accomplishment."
3. "We are always getting ready to live, but never living"
4. "Unless you try to do something beyond what you have already mastered, you will never grow."
5. "The only person you are destined to become is the person you decide to be."
6. "Nothing can bring you peace but yourself"

For more Pearls of Wisdom, please visit our website www.kairosadvisersllc.com/pearls-of-wisdom.

About Pamela J. Thomas

About Pamela J. Thomas

Pamela J. Thomas is the founder, owner and managing advisor of Kairos Advisers LLC. Kairos helps business leaders successfully navigate the challenges in transitioning to retirement. Our proven Retirement Blueprint™ process is designed to clarify their life path and goals and help them map out an exciting, fulfilling retirement, make an impact on the world and leave their legacy.

Through out her life Pam has been a change catalyst, drawing others into seeing broader, more effective possibilities and solutions to the opportunities and challenges in business and in life. This has made her an invaluable partner to business leaders facing major professional and personal transition.

With her authentic, direct approach, she has been instrumental in helping others find the true source of their power and harnessing that power to change their lives and the world around them.

Pam is a generalist and universalist who's ability to scan broadly and discern what is important, find unique connections, synthesize and integrate that information, and, finally, to distill those ideas into tangible strategies to create maximum impact.

Pam has facilitated a variety of workshops, classes, and retreats over the past 15 years for her business and individual clients, including a cutting-edge modality for intuitive training, a method that links the conceptual and intuitive minds.

She is the author of two books *Retirement By Design: How To Pursue Your Passions, Leave Your Legacy and Live The Retirement Of Your Dreams* and *He Restores My Soul: Life Affirming Meditations on the Psalms*.

Pam holds a B.A. in Economics from Princeton University, a M.B.A. in Finance from the Wharton School, and a M. Div. from Union Presbyterian Seminary. She has been a consultant to various individuals, businesses, and other nonprofit organizations for well over a decade.

Prior to starting Kairos Advisers, Pam spent 15 years as an equity analyst, portfolio manager, and consultant for various banks, and investment companies including the Bank of Bermuda, General Electric Investment Corporation (now GE Asset Management) and the Virginia Retirement System.

She is a Chartered Financial Analyst and a Certified Advisor of the Organization for Entrepreneurial Development. She is also a member of Institute of Directors, the UK-based a worldwide association of members that supports, represents and sets standards for corporate directors across the globe. At present, she serves on the Board of Directors of Capital G Bank Ltd. and Capital G Investments Ltd., one of the largest independent integrated financial services organizations in Bermuda.

More About Me

Eclectic is a good word to describe my diverse background and interests. There are two ways to pursue the larger questions of life. The first is to be a specialist and delve deeply into one's chosen field for the answers.

The second is to be a generalist and scan the broad horizon to discern connections and relationships between things. Both perspectives are equally important to our collective pursuit of the "big questions," as one without the other will undoubtedly provide incomplete answers.

I am a generalist. My work has led me to specialize in strategic transformations in organizations.

My clients are entrepreneurs, nonprofit leaders and philanthropists who are seeking innovative ideas to develop business, financial and personal strategies that change lives.

I sit in a unique position to help guide them in clarifying and making decisions about the investment of their time, talents and money and how to make an impact on the world.

At this stage in my life, I am deeply committed to being an agent of constructive transformation in this unique moment in history.

Resources & References

Kairos Advisers LLC helps business leaders successfully overcome the anxiety and dislocation in transitioning to retirement. Our proven process is designed to clarify each individual's life path and goals and help them map out an exciting, fulfilling retirement, make an impact on the world and leave their legacy.

For more information about Pam and Kairos Advisers, please visit:

http://kairosadvisersllc.com

For more detailed information on our Retirement Blueprint™ process, visit:

http://retirement-blueprint.com

You can sign up on this page for a 30-minute complimentary conversation in which we will get started figuring out the timeline and path to get you to your ultimate retirement. There are a limited number of these appointments so schedule now.

Follow us on:

Facebook
www.facebook.com/yourretirementblueprint

Twitter - @retireblueprint

LinkedIn
www.linkedin.com/company/kairos-advisers-llc

Resources & References

Books

Treen, Doug, *Psychology of Executive Retirement: from Fear to Passion*, 2009. Google Books. 2013.

Pink, Daniel, *Drive: The Surprising Truth About What Motivates Us*, 2011. Morehouse Publishing. Amazon Digital Services. 2013.

Peck, M. Scott, *The Road Less Traveled: A New Psychology of Love, Spiritual Growth*. Touchstone Anniversary Edition. Simon & Shuster Digital Sales. 2013.

"Entering the Emptiness" by Gerald May, in *Simpler Living, Compassionate Life: A Christian Perspective*, edited and compiled by Michael Schut, 2009. Amazon Digital Services. 2013.

Graebner, W., *A History Of Retirement: The Meaning And Function Of An American Institution, 1885 to 1978*, Yale University Press 1980.

D. Costa. *The Evolution of Retirement: An American Economic History, 1880-1990*. Chicago, Illinois USA: University of Chicago Press, 1998.

Articles

Dinah Wisenberg Brin, *Do you need a retirement coach?*, CNBC, June 3, 2013.

Richard A. Friedman, *Fast Time and the Aging Mind*, NY Times, July 20, 2013.

Amir Haque, *How To Let Your Purpose Find You*, Harvard Business Review, October 22, 2012.

Reports

US Census Bureau.

Bureau of Labor Statistics.

Social Security Administration.

National Institute on Aging, *Health and Retirement Study: Growing Older in America.*

Employee Benefit Research Institute, *2013 Retirement Confidence Survey.*

The Urban Institute, *Perspectives on Productive Aging.*

Smith & Moen, *Retirement Satisfaction for Retirees and Their Spouses,* Journal of Family Issues, March 2004.

Center for Retirement Research at Boston College, *What Makes Retirees Happy?*

Davis, Guyla D., *Looking Toward the Future: Predicting Retirement Satisfaction*, The New School Psychology Bulletin, Volume 5, No. 1, 2007.

2013 Merrill Lynch Retirement Survey (in partnership with Age Wave), *American's Perspectives on New Retirement Realities and the Longevity Bonus.*

The Cornell Retirement and Well-Being Study, 2000.

2010 Del Webb Baby Boomer Survey.

2013 HSBC The Future of Retirement Survey.

University of Michigan *Growing Old in America: Health & Retirement Study.*

Aegon Retirement Readiness Survey 2013.

Resources & References

The MacArthur Foundation Research Network on an Aging Society.

Families and Work Institute, *2008 National Study of the Changing Workforce.*

AARP 2004 Life Stage Survey.

2013 Merrill Lynch Bank America Workplace Benefits Report.

2013 Mercer Securing Retirement Outcomes Report.

For more Resources and ideas please visit our website www. kairosadvisersllc.com/resources.

www.ingramcontent.com/pod-product-compliance
Lightning Source LLC
Chambersburg PA
CBHW051315170526
45166CB00002B/557